Managing Money
in Higher Education

◆◆◆◆◆◆◆◆◆◆◆◆◆◆◆◆◆◆◆◆◆◆◆◆◆◆◆◆◆◆◆◆◆◆◆◆◆

William E. Vandament

Managing Money
in Higher Education

❖◆❖◆❖◆❖◆❖◆❖◆❖◆❖◆❖◆❖◆❖◆❖◆❖◆❖

A Guide to
the Financial Process
and Effective Participation
Within It

Jossey-Bass Publishers

San Francisco • Oxford • 1989

MANAGING MONEY IN HIGHER EDUCATION
A Guide to the Financial Process and Effective Participation Within It
by William E. Vandament

Copyright © 1989 by: Jossey-Bass Inc., Publishers
350 Sansome Street
San Francisco, California 94104
&
Jossey-Bass Limited
Headington Hill Hall
Oxford OX3 0BW

Library of Congress Cataloging-in-Publication Data

Vandament, William E.
  Managing money in higher education : a guide to the financial
process and effective participation within it / William E.
Vandament.
      p.   cm.—(Jossey-Bass higher education series)
  Includes bibliographical references.
  ISBN 1-55542-192-X
  1. Universities and colleges—Business management.   2. Education,
Higher—Finance.   I. Title.   II. Series.
LB2341.92.V36   1989
378′.02—dc20   89-45577
                                                          CIP

Manufactured in the United States of America

The paper in this book meets the guidelines for
permanence and durability of the Committee on
Production Guidelines for Book Longevity of the
Council on Library Resources.

JACKET DESIGN BY WILLI BAUM

FIRST EDITION

Code 8966

The Jossey-Bass
Higher Education Series

Contents

◆◆◆◆◆◆◆◆◆◆◆◆◆◆◆◆◆◆◆◆◆◆◆◆◆◆◆◆◆◆◆◆◆◆

Foreword, *by Harold L. Enarson*   xi

Preface   xiii

The Author   xix

1. Financial Management in Academic Institutions:
   An Overview   1

2. Assessing Factors That Affect Financial Needs
   and Plans   23

3. Developing a Realistic Budget and Financial Plan 43

4. Managing and Controlling the Flow of Money   63

5. Evaluating and Adjusting the Plan   75

ix

6.   Analyzing Costs and Revenues for Reallocation
     Decisions   94

7.   Building Competence in Financial Planning
     and Management   115

     Glossary of Financial Terms   127

     References   131

     Index   135

Foreword

❖❖❖❖❖❖❖❖❖❖❖❖❖❖❖❖❖❖❖❖❖❖❖❖❖❖❖

To a remarkable degree, the greater part of administration in higher education is the work of amateurs. Professors who enjoyed orderly career progression—graduate student, teaching assistant, assistant professor, senior faculty member—discover that heading a department, a college, an institute, or a program anywhere on campus involves a wrenching change. Administration catapults one into a work environment that can quickly become difficult, bewildering, even dangerous to one's career. Most newly appointed administrators are amateurs—gifted amateurs, but amateurs nonetheless. They have much to learn quickly about leadership and followership, about planning and affirmative action, and especially about the management of money.

    If there were a manual for academic administrators on how to get things done without getting into big trouble, it would stress the importance of financial management and build on the knowledge and insights in *Managing Money in Higher Education*. The literature on financial management is substantial. But however useful it may be for professionals in the field, it is surely forbidding to the typical academic administrator. The unique value of this book is that it is designed to help administrators at all levels develop the financial literacy they need to do their jobs well. It underscores the important but neglected truth that financial management threads throughout the entire organization: It cannot be monopolized by treasurers, comptrollers, and budget and fiscal analysts.

A character in an E. B. White story said, "I predict a bright future for complexity. Have you ever considered how complicated things can get, what with one thing always leading to another?" Financial management is everybody's business, an ever more sophisticated and complicated business. Learning on the job can be costly; administrators who want to be spared the errors others have made will profit from this book. "Book learning" *can* inform decision making, and this book does just that. Readers will increase their financial literacy, gaining a better grasp of the accrual method of accounting, cash management, fixed and variable costs, and—that Pandora's box—the ever present danger of embezzlement. Careers have ended because of failure to observe William Vandament's admonition: "Do not assume that a competent person who works long hours will not steal."

The book is soundly and logically structured and thus invites browsing. Its tone is optimistic. Vandament considers the campus a place of multiple enterprises and likens the department to a small business. He finds creativity both desirable and possible, and he encourages the entrepreneurial spirit. He shows how support services, such as the computer center, often operate as "monopolies" to be placated or outmaneuvered. Vandament offers much wisdom on such matters. Students of higher education will also find value in this book because it puts financial complexity in context and makes it intelligible.

Each chapter is graced with several case studies. These alone make this pioneering book "worth the price of admission."

September 1989   Harold L. Enarson
                                   President Emeritus
                                   The Ohio State University

Preface

❖❖❖❖❖❖❖❖❖❖❖❖❖❖❖❖❖❖❖❖❖❖❖❖❖❖❖❖❖

The financial management of colleges and universities in the
United States has become increasingly sophisticated over the past
two or three decades. Just a few short years ago, the institutional
president wrote the budget on a lined yellow tablet and then turned
over to a trusted bookkeeper the management of the institutional
checking account and disbursement of its funds. But times have
changed. Institutional administrators now must master techniques
developed in business administration in order to manage financial
affairs that are growing increasingly complex.

Despite their nonprofit status, colleges and universities are
among the most diversified enterprises in existence. Most of them
receive income from multiple sources and deliver a variety of services to students and other clients. They maintain facilities and
invest assets that take many forms and that often are segregated
into separate accounts for specialized functions. Even their smallest
program units—academic departments and auxiliary enterprises—
often piece together resources from several sources in an entrepreneurial fashion to fulfill their aspirations and those of their
constituencies.

Purpose of the Book

Managing Money in Higher Education is a primer on financial management for college and university program officers and faculty who have moved from fields other than business into positions of administrative responsibility. Its basic premise is that effective financial management of an institution is the responsibility not only of professional financial staff but also of those who are charged with conducting its programs, including academic and student services vice presidents, deans and program directors, department chairpersons, and faculty participating in academic governance— even presidents and chancellors. Administrators must be ingenious in acquiring funds and in using them to full advantage if they are to guide their programs successfully. These people, often confronting complex financial concepts for the first time, must be informed clients if they are to gain the maximum benefit from the technical expertise of trained financial staff.

The literature on financial management in higher education for business professionals and for those who study higher education administration as a career is growing almost exponentially. In some ways, this expansion of the literature is itself making the task of learning about the subject more difficult for the person assuming responsibility for academic programs or services. Acronyms, esoteric terms, and specialized topics abound; and unguided browsing in the library or responding to book advertisements can often lead the potential reader into unexpected, perhaps unwelcome, territory. As very busy people, many administrators abandon the search for knowledge in the field and hope that they can learn enough to function by remaining alert in the company of those who seem to know what they are doing. I am convinced that there is a better way, and I have sought to demonstrate it in this book.

Overview of the Chapters

The approach taken here is to move one by one through each financial management task faced by the administrator, describing relevant aspects of the processes involved and introducing the concepts underlying sound practices in the task at hand. The introduction, which covers the purposes of financial management and characteristics of the financial management environment in higher education, provides a backdrop against which the practices in subsequent chapters can be measured. It has not been necessary to resort to esoteric terms or concepts to provide that background. Short case studies, each usually describing a situation in which disregard for sound practices has led to problems, are presented throughout the book to illustrate the practical value of the concepts.

In Chapter One I describe the scope of financial management activities and advance the idea that effective management is a collective effort in higher education. The purposes of financial management are presented to illuminate practices that often appear obscure to the naive observer. In addition, I review special characteristics of colleges and universities that distinguish them from other types of organizations in order to put their financial management activities in broader perspective.

Chapter Two describes the process of collecting information on financial issues that must be addressed to further the aspirations of the institution and its units. Stress is placed on using methods that ensure that plans become reality rather than serve as filler for bookshelves or file cabinets.

Chapter Three examines the content and the process of developing a budget and a financial plan. I offer examples of ways creative administrators assemble resources to meet the needs of their programs and suggest an active, entrepreneurial approach to counter the tin-cup posture frequently observed in higher education administrators.

Chapter Four deals with practices for maintaining control of the financial plan so that its purposes are not subverted. These practices address issues ranging from preventing embezzlement and ensuring that the organization gets what it is paying for to responding to unexpected shortages of revenue. Basic purposes underlying control procedures are defined so that administrators can positively influence others and be informed critics if mindless red tape is thwarting program objectives.

Chapter Five suggests criteria for assessing the financial

management plan and process. The fifteen criteria for evaluation are organized within the basic tasks of protecting the asset base, ensuring resources for activities of high priority, and maintaining control while the plan is being executed. The concepts of recurring costs and revenues, annual rate calculations, and accrual-method accounting are introduced, and their utility is demonstrated in case studies.

Chapter Six reviews factors that must be considered in managing costs and revenues. Drawing on recent work by financial managers on cost behavior analysis, the chapter stresses the importance of net cost-revenue relationships in financial and program decisions.

Chapter Seven contains an overview of and selected references for special topics: information technology, financial accounting reports, and fiscal crisis. The chapter presents a general review of the administrator's role in financial management and supports an active approach at all administrative levels in the institution.

Acknowledgments

I wish to acknowledge several people who have contributed directly or indirectly to this book. I am deeply indebted to George Baughman and the late Judith Washburn of The Ohio State University, who maintained a state-of-the-art environment in financial management and contributed greatly to the comprehensive view of financial management I sought to portray in this volume. William Griffith, Elizabeth Knapp, the late Martin Phillips, and Michael Young set excellent examples as professional planners. Scott Hughes and James Hyatt, both former directors of the Financial Management Center of the National Association of College and University Business Officers (NACUBO), charted important directions followed by NACUBO's Financial Management Committee during the late 1970s and the 1980s. I would also like to thank my colleagues on that committee and its task forces for their significant contributions to the field and for their good fellowship.

This volume is dedicated to Margie Vandament, who tirelessly hosted many of the events at which we pursued the quest for

sound financial management and who helped me write in terms
that are more understandable than they otherwise would be.

Signal Hill, California   William E. Vandament
September 1989

The Author

❖❖❖❖❖❖❖❖❖❖❖❖❖❖❖❖❖❖❖❖❖❖❖❖❖❖❖❖❖❖❖

William E. Vandament is a Trustee Professor of the California State University (CSU) system and professor of psychology at California State University, Fullerton. He received a B.A. degree (1952) from Quincy College, an M.S. degree (1953) from Southern Illinois University, and both M.S. (1963) and Ph.D. (1964) degrees from the University of Massachusetts, Amherst, all in psychology.

Prior to assuming his present duties, Vandament served as provost and vice chancellor for academic affairs for the CSU system. Earlier in his career, he was assistant professor of psychology, director of institutional research, and assistant vice president for planning at the State University of New York, Binghamton. He later became executive assistant to the president for budget and resources planning and vice president for finance and planning at The Ohio State University and senior vice president for administration at New York University.

Vandament has served as chairperson of the financial management committee of NACUBO and as a member of the National Center for Higher Education Management Systems' board of directors. He is active in the Council for the Development of Education and is directing its efforts to establish a national registry of higher education reform.

Managing Money
in Higher Education

❖❖❖❖❖❖❖❖❖❖❖❖❖❖❖❖❖❖❖❖❖❖❖❖❖❖❖❖❖❖

One

Financial Management in Academic Institutions: An Overview

❖❖❖❖❖❖❖❖❖❖❖❖❖❖❖❖❖❖❖❖❖❖❖❖❖❖❖❖❖❖❖❖❖

Effective financial management in a college or university comprises a wide range of activities, some requiring specialized skills and others only common sense. Nearly every member of the faculty and staff is involved in financial management in some way. In fact, the college or university can be viewed as a complex economic community in which separate academic departments and administrative units provide services for and receive income from a variety of internal and external consumers. The task of financial management goes far beyond the simple budgeting of available resources; it involves the weaving together of multiple financial plans into a consolidated whole. Therefore, the program administrators in the institution's central administration and in each of its units must understand the basic concepts of financial management if they are to contribute to a total institutional effort.

Scope of Financial Management

Even a partial list of the activities involved in the financial management of colleges and universities can be lengthy. These

1

activities range from the development of major strategic plans to the conscientious collection of minor fees from users. The following list highlights their variety:

Assessing needs for revenue

Seeking funds from outside sources

Making allocation decisions and establishing agreements for services by units

Establishing revenue targets and strategies for departments and units

Maintaining a productive investment program

Controlling fraud and embezzlement

Designing energy-efficient buildings

Directing programs to achieve efficiency and reduce waste

Operating a cash management program to gain interest income

Negotiating favorable contracts with vendors and employees

Timing vendor payments to receive discounts

Maintaining buildings and other capital assets

Retaining and developing good faculty

Controlling expenditures in accordance with plans

Fixing leaky faucets and running toilets

Ensuring that only authorized personnel make purchases

Collecting fees in a timely manner

Maintaining appropriate inventories of supplies

Assessing space utilization and requirements

Providing timely income and expenditure information to program officers

Saving waste paper for recycling programs

Entertaining or sending a birthday card to an important donor

Evaluating financial plans for future revision

Enforcing parking regulations and other rules

Adjusting department budgets to changing conditions

Establishing indirect cost rates for sponsored projects

Bringing in capital projects within their budgets

Searching for alternative ways of providing services

Clearly, the heads of all departments and offices are financial managers who must develop and administer financial plans and ensure that the plans are followed and that waste is kept at low levels within their units. At an individual level, the faculty member who turns off unneeded lights or puts trash in appropriate containers is contributing to effective financial management, as is the library assistant who tracks down overdue books with a vengeance, or the bookstore clerk who makes the elimination of shoplifting a personal mission.

In many institutions, unfortunately, financial management is regarded as the exclusive domain of the professional financial management staff. Some of the fiscal staff themselves may see the importance only of their own areas of special expertise and give a low priority to the broader set of activities necessary for effective management. However, an institution will achieve effective financial management only when there is a collective awareness of the roles that individuals play in its financial health.

According to Miles's first maxim, where you stand depends on where you sit (Miles, 1978, p. 399); a person's view of issues is contingent on his or her position in an organization. On the one hand, in a college or university, a senior administrator may focus on the way unrestricted institutional funds are acquired and distributed across the departments and offices of the institution. Departmental or unit managers, on the other hand, may define the task of financial management as one of piecing together revenues from several sources, including allocations from the institution's unrestricted general fund, to accomplish a set of objectives that overlaps those of the institution but also contains some goals specific to each unit. Effective institutional management requires the reconciliation and integration of both views.

A single academic department may resemble a small business engaged in several related activities, each generating revenues and entailing obligations for services. Its financial management plan thus represents the integration of a set of arrangements for providing revenues and consuming human or material resources. The allocation to the department from the institution's unrestricted general fund usually carries obligations for providing instruction to enrolled students; often it includes vaguely described obligations for faculty research and participation in institutional governance. In some large private universities each academic unit's allocation may be tied directly to the tuition and gift revenue generated by its instructional program; in this case the term *allocation* reflects only a bookkeeping procedure to describe an institutional franchise for what is essentially a self-sufficient business.

The department may depend on grants and contracts to its faculty from external sources. These subsidize faculty salaries, provide graduate student support, and furnish equipment needed by the department. However, these sources may entail the release of faculty from some teaching responsibilities and require the dedication of space in which to conduct the research or other service for which the grant or contract was awarded. The department may also rely on gifts and endowments to fund a portion of its programs. These funds are sometimes accompanied by extra service commitments in areas that would otherwise receive a lower priority in the department. Finally, the department may sell services that generate income from user fees and require either direct expenditures or the release of faculty and staff from other responsibilities; such services include theatrical or musical performances, professional workshops or conferences, and medical practices.

As diversified small (and, in some cases, not so small) businesses, academic schools and departments and some administrative support units face many of the trade-offs among costs, revenues, and services that are customarily associated with the private sector. For example, in accepting a major research contract in a specialized area, a department may need to divert resources that currently support individual faculty efforts on several topics.

Many colleges and universities have a large number of these educational enterprises operating in what may resemble a municipality or economic community. These units, while sharing some educational missions, are usually encouraged to pursue individual goals to enrich their programs and the institution as a whole. They typically are monitored by the institutional administration, however, to ensure that their entrepreneurial activities are not inconsistent or in competition with their responsibilities to the institution and that they can meet their commitments to others without placing undue burdens on the institution.

The institution also maintains several organizations that serve as public utilities for its community, providing services to students and the academic departments. Among them are the library, the computer center, the admissions and registrar's offices, residence and dining halls, the bookstore, and reproduction and publication centers. These support operations often function as monopolies and thus require institutional oversight like that provided by regulatory commissions in the public sector to ensure that services are adequate and that prices are reasonable. These operations must also be led by administrators with considerable expertise in administration and financial management.

Viewed from this perspective, then, the financial management task at the central, institutional level is to coordinate a complex economic community as well as administer the core set of funds that flow directly to the institution as a whole. The responsibilities of the central administration range from monitoring the health of the individual units and controlling their trade with one another to allocating centrally administered funds. The college or university's financial plan thus represents the consolidation of unit plans that are themselves the result of the integration of many components. It is an economic plan for accomplishing broad, shared objectives and the separate goals of the many individual units and people who make commitments on behalf of, and with the franchise of, the institution.

Purposes of Financial Management

An early task of the administrator in an academic setting is to find out what activities constitute financial management within his or her sphere and then to determine what personal responsibilities they entail. However, the quest for a basic statement of financial management purposes can be frustrating to the person untrained in business affairs. Many financial administrators have gained their expertise by mastering specific aspects of financial management in the absence of overarching concepts; much of the shared knowledge that makes up their expertise, unfortunately, has not been specifically articulated.

Indeed, as late as 1981 the Financial Management Committee

of the National Association of College and University Business Officers (NACUBO) embarked on a project to define financial management in higher education and to compile some principles of its sound practice. The task turned out to be far more complicated than anticipated because of the absence of a comprehensive literature on the subject. The financial neophyte therefore should not be embarrassed or discouraged if at first some of the practices of financial management appear inscrutable or their purposes difficult to comprehend.

The task force formed by the NACUBO committee was surprised to find that existing writings on financial management stressed relatively narrow sets of activities, avoiding broad concepts. To some writers, investment management and the accumulation of capital are the key elements of financial management. To others, primarily in the field of higher education, financial management is almost synonymous with the budgeting of expenditures; little reference is made to the generation of revenue. Still others stress financial accounting and controlling; indeed, the accounting profession is evolving new approaches that will contribute to the more effective management of resources in business as well as institutions of higher learning. However, there is more to financial management than cutting-edge accounting, strategic budgeting, or managing investments.

Writers in the academic discipline of finance give varied treatments to the term *financial management*. For example, Brigham (1987) treats financial management as one of three areas of financial activity (the others being money and capital markets and investments) and gives it limited coverage, considering it a part of "decisions within the firm" (p. 4). Rao (1987, p. 6) provides a succinct view of financial management in the business sector: "The goal of financial management must be to maximize the price of the company's stock." This statement suggests that a company with effective financial management will carry out a wide variety of activities—such as multiple product development and marketing, cost containment, and revenue production—in ways that produce profits while maintaining its potential for long-range health to attract potential investors.

Clearly, the concept of financial management is something

to be designed rather than discovered. It is not a fact of nature but a set of activities created by humans to serve useful purposes. One cannot simply define financial management as "what financial managers do" or as merely acquiring money and spending it. Neither definition carries enough information to aid the administrator who is working to put resources together to accomplish an organization's mission. NACUBO's task force, having searched the literature with only limited success, finally adopted the approach to language advocated by Humpty Dumpty in *Through the Looking Glass, and What Alice Found There:* "When I use a word, it means just what I wish it to mean—neither more, nor less" (Gardner, 1960, p. 269). The task force created its own concept of financial management. "Financial management in a college or university is necessary in order to accomplish the following objectives: 1. To help ensure, to the extent possible, that the valued institutional activities of instruction, research, and public service are supported by adequate resources; 2. To help protect the ability of the institution to continue its activities through the sound management, control, and investment of its financial resources; 3. To help promote the efficient and effective management of existing resources through sound planning and budgeting and responsible stewardship" (Hyatt and Santiago, 1986, p. 2).

This broad statement of purposes encompasses nearly every action within an organization that involves the acquisition or use of resources; thus it treats financial management as the responsibility of nearly every member of the faculty and administration of a college or university. The definition of financial management used in this book adopts the premise that financial management is a comprehensive set of activities, involving nearly every institutional officer, directed toward meeting program needs and achieving long-range institutional health.

The fundamental purposes underlying all sound financial management practices are few and may appear self-evident to a fresh observer who has not participated in a prolonged search for them. Yet in practice, their relationship to actual procedures and policies can become blurred with the passage of time. Financial practices can then come to resemble cultural traditions that are followed blindly in an effort to placate forces of nature that are not fully understood. Institutions that undertake a review of paperwork involving financial transactions often find forms and procedures that are unnecessary to meet management objectives, sometimes without a written description of their origins.

In fact, a blind institutional devotion to existing methods of doing business can discourage the creation of ways to meet new situations or to address old problems more effectively. Practices designed to meet the issues of one era or set of conditions may become so entrenched that their successful execution becomes the standard by which financial management is measured, even when they are no longer appropriate to the institution's needs. Therefore, the administrator who understands the fundamental purposes of financial management not only can become adept at managing resources but also can become an informed client of the technical staff that provides financial services to the institution and its units.

The fundamental purposes of financial management advanced in this book (differing slightly from those of the NACUBO task force) are these:

1. The long-range protection and enhancement of the organization's ability to accomplish its missions
2. The provision of adequate resources to support the present valued activities of the organization
3. The maintenance of accountability to those organizational constituencies with a stake in the organization's services

These fundamental purposes do not make explicit reference to some factors, mentioned in the NACUBO statement, that are commonly assumed to be vital to financial management, such as efficiency, cost containment, and productivity. Such Calvinist values are treated here as derivative conditions of the fundamental purposes of financial management that become significant only when resources are limited. Most (but not all) institutions and program units operate with limited revenues and must therefore try to achieve economies. However, a blind obedience to these virtues as primary goals requiring no further justification can actually undermine an organization's long-range potential. For example, if an institution requires sacrifices that its employees perceive to be unnecessary or unduly severe, it may deplete its human resource base and undermine morale. In short, the struggle to achieve efficiency is usually a necessary part of meeting the fundamental purposes of financial management, but efficiency is not a fundamental purpose itself.

On the other hand, maintaining accountability to the institution's constituencies is regarded in this book as a fundamental purpose of financial management. One might argue that an institution and its separate units maintain accountability only as a self-serving device to gain revenues for their current and future activities. That argument, however, assumes that the welfare of the institution or a program unit takes precedence over all other interests, including the organization's missions and the services that it provides to its constituencies. In making accountability a fundamental purpose, the author assumes that the mission and associated services themselves hold primacy and that the institution or unit must demonstrate to its constituencies that maintaining its health is the best way to ensure that those missions are fulfilled.

Protecting and Enhancing Organizational Ability. In general, the actions taken to fulfill this purpose protect the institution's or program unit's future capacity to generate necessary revenues and avoid unmanageable costs. Ideally, they will enhance future revenue generation and reduce future costs. This purpose of financial management has been met for a given period if the organization's asset base has remained stable or improved and if its recurring or future obligations have remained stable or been reduced.

Necessary organizational assets are both tangible and intangible; they include endowments or reserve funds, facilities, equipment, the quality of faculty and staff, the quality and attractiveness of programs, and the confidence of public or private sources on which the institution or unit must rely for future funding. Many actions must be taken to protect and improve these assets and thus to preserve the organization's ability to provide needed services and produce adequate revenues for future operation. For example, the institution's budget must be balanced so that fund balances are not reduced during the fiscal year. Endowment expenditure policies must preserve the principal's real value, adjusted for inflation. Preventive maintenance and plant modernization must be carried out regularly and funds put aside for future replacement or major rehabilitation. As with any business, the "product line" and the "brand name"—the institution's programs and its reputation—must be nurtured so that they will be useful and marketable in the future; therefore, high-quality faculty and staff, on which the educational program depends, must be retained and developed.

Meanwhile, commitments to major expenditures in the absence of identified revenues to support them must be avoided; current debt must be reduced if possible. The uncontrolled expansion or proliferation of programs can strain an asset base that is not growing commensurately. The acceptance of gifts or grants can sometimes carry excessive expenditure obligations far into the future.

In sum, long-range organizational health depends on the protection of an adjusted asset base—one in which assets have been reconciled with future obligations. An organization predicting a stable-state future can be content to protect its current base; one aspiring to expand or improve quality must correspondingly expand or improve its base.

Supporting Valued Activities. The basic financial concerns of the here and now are generating adequate income and distributing resources among activities in accordance with organizational priorities. Because resources are usually limited, their efficient use is an important part of program support.

The quest for revenues seems never-ending in most institutions. It involves developing strong justification for outside sources of funds (for example, government officials and potential donors), active cash management programs to ensure that interest income is high, pricing strategies for consumers of services, relentless collection programs for funds due the institution or program unit, investment strategies that balance risk and yield, and strong development programs. At times it involves the investment of resources in programs such as public affairs and governmental relations, where the relationship of investment to income generation is not direct.

Funds acquired must be applied in a manner that matches the institution's priorities and the needs of its programs. Therefore, priorities among competing activities and the resource requirements of each of those activities must be clearly defined. A clear link between planning and budgeting must exist; that is, the budget must represent the implementation of plans, and the programs' resource needs must be analyzed before resources are distributed. This analysis must take into account not only the obvious staffing requirements but also the full range of resources—such as facilities, equipment, and supplies—required to support the programs.

Efficiency is important because available resources normally do not exceed program needs. During shortages, of course, waste in one program deprives another program of resources or undermines the institution's ability to protect its asset base for the future. For most organizations, therefore, the pursuit of efficiency must assume a high priority as a means of providing adequate support for programs. Approaches to reducing costs sometimes involve the rationing of resources, such as supplies or staff; in this case ongoing activities are accomplished without change in the basic method of delivery. Other approaches involve significant changes in the way services are provided, such as consolidation of fragmented support operations or contracting for services with outside agents. Effective financial management typically includes a never-ending search for ways to reduce costs while maintaining quality in the organization's services.

Maintaining Accountability. The institution and its program units operate in order to accomplish several missions that are important to its constituencies—the provision of education, the creation of knowledge, the assistance of the broader community through the assemblage of specialized talents. It is the institution's responsibility to provide information to its constituencies as they weigh their priorities and make decisions about the best ways to obtain services, those provided by the college or university as well as those provided by other organizations. The unnecessary consumption of resources by the college or university may deprive other activities that are valued by the broader public, such as public safety or health. The public must, therefore, be served by prudent financial management and by the provision of information sufficient for it to make informed decisions. Institutional advocacy is appropriate only to the extent that it is informative and backed by commitments to provide services effectively. These accountability requirements also apply to each of the program units in its dealings with the institutional administration and other constituencies.

Factors in Higher Education Management

Although the following factors are not unique to higher education, they differentiate its financial management from that of many other private and public organizations. Fund accounting, joint products, nonprofit status, a utopian financial philosophy, and professionalism present a rare blend of complexity, constraints, and opportunities.

Fund Accounting. Most colleges and universities rely on multiple sources of income to support their programs. Unlike the revenues of a typical business, which can be pooled from all sources for any use, the revenues of colleges and universities often come with restrictions on their use and must be segregated in budget and accounting reports. Unrestricted general funds—usually derived from state appropriations, tuition and general fees, unrestricted gifts, and income from unrestricted endowments—are customarily pooled because the restrictions on their use are minimal. However, the institution's budget and financial statements and those of its program units usually contain also a lengthy series of restricted fund accounts for which expenditure conditions have been specified by the external funding agency or donor.

These restricted fund accounts vary greatly in the extent to which they provide support for the institution's core programs. Sometimes the donor specifies that the funds be used for activities that would be carried on anyway; in this case, the restricted funds can be treated as an offset to unrestricted funds. In other cases, the restrictions require services beyond those normally covered by unrestricted funds; the two types of funds thus are not interchangeable. Customary accounting practices do not differentiate between restricted funds that can be used for general purposes and those that cannot. Thus financial planning sometimes involves keeping informal records when restricted funds are used selectively to support general fund activities.

Operations charging clients for services can also generate earnings that are not entirely interchangeable with unrestricted funds. Where an operation is officially designated as an auxiliary enterprise—such as residence halls, the bookstore, and the athletics department—revenues and expenditures must be segregated from other institutional resources. For many of these operations, this segregation is necessary to meet obligations to those who have purchased bonds secured by the assets or the promise of future income of the auxiliary operation. In other cases, internal management agreements have been reached between the institution's board or administration and the operation to ensure that the operation does not become a drain on unrestricted funds and to provide an incentive for prudent management by allowing the operation to use its surplus revenues for its own improvements or long-range financial security.

The financial management of colleges and universities is made more complex by the existence of these restricted and designated funds. The use of formal fund accounting techniques helps clarify matters but often falls short of providing useful information on the informal interchangeability of funds among categories.

Joint Products. A single activity of a faculty member may serve multiple purposes. For example, the supervision of a graduate thesis may simultaneously provide an educational experience for a student and contribute to the university's research program. While assuming responsibility for an internship experience, a faculty member may also be conducting research and providing public service.

The joint-product nature of higher education, of course, makes separate judgments about productivity and the costs of programs difficult. Should the cost of a doctoral thesis be charged solely or in part to the instructional program, or should it be regarded as the cost of research, with the student's contribution considered a partial subsidy of the research program? The fact that joint products are common in higher education also can make predictions about the impact of administrative or financial decisions difficult. For example, a reduction in the size of the graduate program will hamper the research effort or actually increase its cost.

On the other hand, the joint-product nature of higher education offers opportunities for program enrichment through grants, contracts, and gifts whose purposes overlap those of the institution. The research grant, for example, often provides student aid, faculty expertise, and equipment that enrich the instructional program and spreads the administrative overhead costs of operating the institution over a larger base. The capable manager searches constantly for external funding opportunities that can serve multiple institutional or unit purposes.

Nonprofit Status. As nonprofit institutions, colleges and universities acquire financial support from outside sources and their consumers largely by demonstrating financial need. At times, sound financial management can reduce the institution's apparent need and thus can actually hamper the process of generating revenues. This often creates a built-in disincentive for sound financial management, since it may undermine the institution's or the program unit's quest to protect its future resource base. Particularly damaging to the institution's future revenue base are one-time surpluses—due perhaps to the delayed start of a program or a short-lived increase in interest rates on investments—that may be mistakenly interpreted by outside agencies as a basic positive change in the institution's financial health.

Of course, this problem is not restricted to dealings with external agencies. At the various administrative levels within the institution the same conflicting objectives are found. Every career bureaucrat in government service knows that funds unspent in one fiscal year will reduce appropriations in subsequent years, and tends to spend accordingly. The department chairperson is reluctant to let the dean see unspent allocations; the dean, in turn, usually tries to demonstrate to the vice president that the school or college is living on the edge of insolvency.

A direct approach to this problem is to forge agreements or understandings with those responsible for allocations about appropriate levels of reserve funds and to formulate explicit plans for the use of savings that can be generated during a given fiscal period.

Just to be on the safe side, however, many financial managers disguise meager reserve funds by converting them into assets that have limited visibility, such as inventories of supplies, earlier-than-planned purchases of equipment and library acquisitions, and transfers to categories of plant fund assets that are not expected to turn over regularly in congruence with fiscal year designations. It is indeed a talented manager or administrator who can effectively manage current funds without undermining the organization's ability to generate resources.

Utopian Financial Philosophy. In the typical college or university, each academic or administrative unit is expected to generate as high a level of resources as possible for the fiscal health of the whole and to require community or institutional support only to the extent that it cannot generate its own resources. Indeed, even the individual faculty members in many academic departments work to obtain outside funding in the form of grants and contracts that will reduce departmental fiscal obligations or provide equipment or other resources to aid the department as a whole. Thus, science departments in a research university are expected to provide support for graduate students largely through grants and contracts from outside agencies, whereas humanities programs rely heavily on institutional support for such purposes. Because their instructional methods are less expensive, schools of business and management often generate more tuition income or state support than they consume. In most medical schools, clinical departments may be expected to support themselves through their practices and perhaps to contribute to the support of basic science departments.

One's view of this utopian approach depends on one's position in the institution. To the institution's or program unit's leaders, these practices appear reasonable and justified. The health of the whole organization is a necessary condition for the strength of any of the parts, including departments and persons that make major financial contributions to the community effort. The institution's leaders consider the revenue potential of departments and people to be derived primarily from their association with the college or university and regard their contributions as appropriate compensation for the organization's franchise to practice their professions. Programs and departments that generate significant revenues, however, sometimes complain that such taxation deprives them of opportunities to improve their programs and undermines incentives for the production of revenue. In the end, compromises with the basic utopian approach are usually made.

Professionalism. The faculty, the key staff of the college or university, is composed of people who possess specialized expertise exceeding that of the people charged with administering the institution. Thus the administrator making allocation decisions must often rely for justification or specification of needs on the technical expertise of the very person seeking the funds. This conflict of interest—like that found in medicine or law, where the person advising on surgery or litigation is the person who will benefit financially from its execution—is characteristic of all professions. Although personal income is not customarily involved in these higher education decisions, their complexity is magnified by the fact that faculty members are loyal not only to their institutions but to their disciplines and can be expected to be disciplinary advocates.

As difficult as this conflict may be for the academic administrator on a day-to-day basis, it can be worsened by the professional accreditation process. Accrediting teams frequently recommend increased institutional expenditures for the program in question—to reduce the student-faculty ratio, increase funding for research, provide additional facilities and equipment, and so forth. Most institutions are unable to comply with the aggregated recommendations for additional funding presented by all accrediting bodies; at the same time, their administrators lack the technical knowledge to assure themselves that their priorities for the expenditure of limited funds have been totally informed. Since this problem is endemic, most academic administrators rely on a blend of natural skepticism about funding requests from the program units with attempts to develop a collegial environment whose members can rise above parochial interests and assist in differentiating higher- and lower-priority concerns.

Division of Financial Responsibilities

The responsibilities for the financial management of a college or university are distributed broadly among the heads of the institution's academic and administrative units. Successful financial management requires these responsibilities to be defined clearly as they are delegated so that the separate activities of the units may be coordinated in common service to the overall plan.

Colleges and universities vary widely in the emphasis they place on the coordination of these separate activities. In some private universities—usually large institutions that emphasize graduate studies and research—each academic unit functions with few central support services and is expected to manage its own financial affairs in a manner that will not place burdens on the remainder of the institution. In other institutions, resource acquisition and allocation are the responsibility of the campus or system administration, and the coordination and line administration of financial management activities are highly centralized.

Chief Financial Officer. Whatever the degree of financial management centralization, most U.S. colleges and universities have one or more officers whose primary responsibility is to coordinate the financial management activities of the various units and to administer central financial management services—budgeting, controlling expenditures, distributing periodic financial information to administrators, investing resources, and purchasing. In some cases, a single chief fiscal officer—a vice president for finance or a vice president for business and administration—has primary responsibility for integrating these activities. In other institutions, the central responsibilities are divided among two or more officers, one dealing with budgeting and planning and the other with technical aspects of financial control and investment.

Institution-wide responsibility for financial management coordination, although common today in the United States, would have been considered radical in the traditional European universities, where confederations of faculty provided instruction and individually collected fees. Even today, the existence of financial administrators at the level of vice president or vice-chancellor is rare in universities outside the United States. The elevated position of financial administrators in American higher education reflects changing aspirations for financial management in these institutions. Earlier expectations did not go beyond simple stewardship of funds; the financial manager's role was limited primarily to collecting, keeping records of, and disbursing funds. As institutions developed in the United States, diversifying sources of revenues and a growing awareness of the opportunities afforded by a more active financial management led to increased complexity and created the need for specialized services.

Today, the institution's chief financial officer or team of officers typically is responsible for the following activities:

- Line administration of the central offices engaged in financial management services—the offices of planning, budgeting, the treasurer, the bursar, accounting and accounts payable, and others.
- Advising the institution's chief executive on financial management matters.
- Coordinating the financial management activities of the separate academic and administrative units.
- Providing leadership and education in effective financial management for all of the institution's academic and administrative units.
- Administering a variety of services indirectly related to institution-wide financial management—plant operation and maintenance, security, facilities design and construction, personnel services, and the computer center.

The chief financial officer frequently coordinates the financial activities of many departments and offices without direct line authority or responsibility for their general operation. The ambiguity created by these arrangements mandates that the chief academic officer, as well as other senior administrators, maintain a close working relationship with the financial officer to protect his or her own administrative program prerogatives while promoting the general financial health that is crucial to the quality of the academic programs. A healthy tension may characterize this relationship, but an institution gains considerably from the presence of strong persons in both positions when they can engage in free and open discourse on the trade-offs that are inevitable in any financial plan or action.

The financial staff often provide an invaluable professional service as consultants or advisers to administrators. When the financial leadership of an institution makes this role a high priority, a client-professional relationship between program and fiscal staff can be developed that is beneficial to all concerned. This advisory role is not often made explicit in organizational mission statements or in position descriptions. It nonetheless can be one of the most important and rewarding components of service for staff in the institution's fiscal offices.

Program Administrators. The academic administrators of the institution—the chief academic officer and staff, deans, department chairs, program directors—must consider the management of financial affairs for the units under their supervision to be a significant portion of their responsibilities. These officers must engage in sophisticated planning as they link program objectives to multiple sources of funds and the commitments incurred in obtaining those funds. A chief fiscal officer and a technical staff are useful to the academic officer in these endeavors; however, their usefulness is sometimes limited by their lack of knowledge about the specific educational issues involved in the many academic programs of the campus or the market factors governing the availability of external funds in narrowly defined program areas and the conditions under which those funds can be negotiated. For this reason, in some colleges and universities the chief academic officer, as executive vice president or provost, actually oversees the financial planning of the institution with the assistance of the chief financial officer and staff.

A natural tendency of many academic or program administrators is to relinquish financial management decisions to the technical fiscal staff because they seem extraneous or baffling. This forfeiting may be made easier by the willingness of fiscal staff to assume those responsibilities. However, a college or university with program administrators inept in financial affairs is likely to find that its program aspirations are often thwarted and that there never seems to be a viable way of accomplishing financial transactions that further valued objectives. In such instances, one hears much castigation of the "bean counters" who are running the institution; in fact, a closer investigation may well reveal that the cause of the difficulty resides in academic staff who are not motivated or informed enough to make productive use of a technical staff that has good, but narrowly defined, expertise.

Thus, an effective academic administrator at an institutional level or in a program unit must not only possess many of the financial skills required to run a small, diversified business; that administrator should also have sufficient acquaintance with the professional aspects of financial management to be an informed client for the services that can be provided by the technical staff. Indeed, the administrator must understand basic concepts in several financial areas—the objectives and nature of the expenditure control process, the accrual basis of accounting, cash management programs, and so forth—to communicate properly with that staff and ask questions that will provide relevant and helpful responses.

Faculty. Most colleges and universities provide a significant consultative role for the faculty in the financial management process. After all, the faculty is the key professional staff in higher education and its expertise in defining priorities for support of academic programs must be sought, particularly in the financial planning process. For example, the faculty can play a major role in the consideration of various trade-offs that must be made in most institutions—between instructional equipment replacement, clerical support, library acquisitions, class section sizes, instructional computer support, and so on. In fact, one can draw many parallels between the administration of a college or university and the management of a professional practice group in medicine or law.

At the same time, however, higher education institutions operate with a franchise, and often with fiscal support, from broader public bodies to which they are accountable through boards of trustees or regents via the institution's administration. This means, of course, that the administration may at times find itself caught between the conflicting interests of its professional staff and its recognized governing board or government officials representing the interests of the public at large. The administrator who successfully bridges the gulf that exists between interested parties at such times is indeed skilled.

In general, an active consulting role for an institution's faculty not only leads to more informed decisions but also can create a climate that allows for the resolution of conflict with less damage to the institution. As one faculty member states: "I don't mind being in on the emergency landing as long as I have been party to the take-off." Customary forms of faculty participation in the financial management process are institution-wide committees on budget or planning, department or school deliberations, and advisory committees for special areas, such as the library or computer center. Faculty members participating in financial planning processes, however, must be prepared for the task and must understand the fundamental purposes of financial management and many of the techniques used to achieve it. For this reason it is usually wise to arrange multi-year, staggered terms for faculty members on these committees to provide continuity and informed leadership.

Case Studies

The following examples illustrate practices that appear to further financial management objectives but in fact only make matters more complicated or obscure for administrators. While introducing the mysteries of budgeting, Meisinger and Dubeck (1984) relate the story of the young lion in the zoo who was fed hay day after day while a neighboring old lion was given juicy steaks. When the young lion complained, the old one calmly replied: "Kid, there's been no mistake here. It's just that you're being carried on the budget as a zebra." In the cases that follow, one suspects that the administrators involved would have found a way to trade hay for steaks.

The Academic Two-Step. A state university system maintains line-item control over most aspects of its campuses' budgets and prohibits the transfer of funds between most categories and objects of expenditures. The reason is to maintain accountability and ensure that expenditures are made for the purposes that were approved at the state level. The state budget analyst sums it up clearly: "You said you needed the money for that purpose. How do you now come to the conclusion that you don't? If you needed it more for another purpose, why didn't you work it out with us when we reviewed your budget request? If you don't need it for its agreed-upon purpose, just turn it back to us." In fact, there is nearly a two-year delay between the preparation of budget requests and the start of the fiscal year in question. Unanticipated problems and opportunities often arise in the interim.

Among the transfers prohibited are transfers of funds between objects of expenditure (such as supplies and services or equipment purchase) within each of the major organizational categories (instruction, institutional support, and student services). Because it is possible, however, to transfer funds between organizational categories without specifying the object of expenditure in the receiving unit, the science departments of several campuses have devised a system of transferring supplies and services money to other campus units; these units then purchase unbudgeted equipment for the science departments. The science faculty members remain unrepentant about the subversion of budget controls, noting ruefully that operating their academic programs is more important than obeying a rigid bureaucracy.

Let's Make a Deal. The unspent funds allocated to a public university revert annually to the state treasury. Naturally, there is a major effort to spend all funds during the closing months of each fiscal year, and purchase orders flood the administrative offices. The library director sees an opportunity in this situation and makes the academic vice president an offer that is immediately accepted. The library will move up its planned acquisition schedule a few months to use up unexpended funds from other parts of the university, and it will have its budget for the next year reduced by 70 percent of the amount it consumes during the cupboard-emptying activity of the current year. The library's acquisition budget is thereby enriched and the academic vice president, using the repayment of the current year's discounted "loan" by the library and the subsequent year's budget allocation, pieces together enough money to undertake a major improvement that would not have been possible under strict application of the hand-to-mouth annual budget process.

Two

Assessing Factors
That Affect
Financial Needs and Plans

❖❖❖❖❖❖❖❖❖❖❖❖❖❖❖❖❖❖❖❖❖❖❖❖❖

To attain the goals of obtaining resources and spending them wisely, most institutions move through four phases. These phases must occur in sequence if the institution and its units are to construct financial plans that are responsive to the internal and external environments and that can serve as a clear road map for successful execution. The phases of financial management are these:

1. Projecting needs, opportunities, and factors that make it necessary to adjust existing financial plans
2. Creating the financial management plan for a fiscal year and plans for future years
3. Managing and controlling the plan
4. Assessing the effectiveness of the plan and the financial management process itself in achieving the institution's goals

In practice, the four phases overlap. In many institutions, the central administration is simultaneously projecting needs for year X+2 and beyond, creating the plan for year X+1, controlling the plan for year X, and assessing the plans of years X and X-1.

This chapter contains descriptions of the elements involved in the first phase, making projections of significant factors affecting short- and long-range financial plans. Chapters Three, Four, and Five deal with the other three phases and present recommendations for criteria for evaluating an organization's plan.

Projecting Needs, Opportunities, and Adjustments

Periodic forecasts must be made of the demand for institutional programs and services, their resource requirements, and their income potential. The institution and each of its program units should be continuously exploring new ways of conducting its affairs and surveying changes in the environment that may provide new avenues for service. Before developing financial plans, therefore, the institution must consider factors not under organizational control—such as demographics, accreditation requirements, inflation rates, and investment yield rates—as well as factors that may be affected by internal decisions—such as enrollment limits, new directions taken by institutional program units, and changes in academic programs or policies.

It is recommended that the institution and each of its units create its own checklist of information related to its unique financial decisions and conduct a formal inventory and review of those items before beginning to construct new financial plans. For some categories of information—such as demographics, inflation rates, and interest rates—the potential financial effects can be quantified within ranges and entered directly into simulated financial scenarios to be used in the formal development of the financial management plans. In other instances, scanning of both external and internal environments may lead to the development of proposed actions that then can be entered into financial simulations to generate cost and revenue projections. For example, if study results indicate a demand for a new program, proposals might be developed that require subsequent analysis of cost and revenue effects.

Factors Not Under Institutional Control. These factors involve the active participation of many offices in the institution. Therefore, their study requires clear understanding about the delegation of study responsibilities and a method of coordination. Environmental factors include the demographic characteristics of students currently being served and information about the characteristics of students in other institutions, which can be used in a search for new student markets or clearer delineation of targeted markets; trends in students' course and major preferences, career choices, and employment opportunities; changes in other institutions' program offerings or admissions and other enrollment-related policies; projected inflation rates; trends in interest rates and changing investment opportunities or dangers; projected changes in construction and land acquisition costs and market values of current capital assets; projections of state and federal revenues to be utilized by the institution or its students; and inventories of the future obligations, increased revenue potential, and savings that flow from prior institutional decisions and actions.

Factors Affected Directly by Institutional Decisions. The cost and revenue effects of factors that can be controlled by the institution also must be determined prior to creating financial plans that will support future activities. These factors may be in response to opportunities and challenges in the external environment or motivated solely by internal assessments concluding that changes are desirable. The factors under institutional control include enrollment goals and actions taken to reach them, such as a decision to restrict enrollments or engage in more active marketing; changes in admission standards that may diminish or increase enrollments and workloads, including those associated with remedial instruction; academic program changes, such as the addition or deletion of programs and the restriction or expansion of their size or scope; changes in academic policies for such matters as credit hour, course, or grade point requirements for graduation that might affect enrollments and workloads; changes in endowment income distribution policies and rates to maintain appropriate levels of principal despite inflation and changing yields; investment strategy changes to produce higher yields or reduce risk; development initiative changes that require up-front investment or produce increased revenues from fund-raising activities; programs to increase the income potential of units, including, for example, charges for services and recovery of overhead costs; personnel actions regarding compensation levels, size of staff, and so on; and administrative initiatives to achieve efficiency, economy, or improvements in services, for example, contracting for services, decentralizing support operations, or expanding computer services.

It is assumed that all parts of the institution will be continuously engaged in self-study on the scope and quality of their services and on ways to achieve their objectives more effectively and efficiently. Under some circumstances these review activities may be so diverse and numerous that—unless special efforts are made at the central institutional level—their results are likely not to be recorded formally and not to be incorporated into the institution's planning. Ideally, the institution's administration will create a systematic inventory of these review activities that will serve as the basis for simulated projections of institutional revenue and expenditure alternatives before the budget planning process is begun for a given year.

Role of Program Administrators. Although the institution's central administration must assume the major responsibility for developing information on factors that have institution-wide effects and for integrating planning information from the separate units, the administrators of the individual program areas must also play an active role in information collection and analysis. Full participation in the college or university's planning offers an opportunity for department, office, and division heads to advance the interests of their programs by calling attention to special opportunities or problems in their areas. The program administrator whose participation in the institutional budgeting process consists only of minimal responses to direct institutional inquiries for information will often find that minimal attention has been given his or her program in the planning and budgeting process.

A program unit's operation is affected by many of the uncontrollable external factors that affect the institution as a whole (such as inflation, interest rates, and state revenues) as well as by institution-wide strategies that may be beyond the control of the unit (such as program priorities, faculty and staff compensation, and charge-back rates for central services). At the same time, however, there are additional controllable and uncontrollable factors that are specific to each of the program areas; these must also be analyzed prior to participation in the development of the institution's financial plan. The effective program administrator will create a checklist of unit-specific issues that is reviewed at the appropriate stages in the planning process to ensure that all relevant items have received consideration within the unit and by the institution's central administration. The following elements are a few that should be considered:

- prices of goods and services that are specific to the unit, such as books, journals, specialized materials, and supplies
- status of equipment, including needed replacement because of wear or obsolescence, and costs associated with replacement, augmentation, and maintenance
- human resource requirements to meet program commitments
- compensation and working conditions required to maintain or achieve a competitive position in the hiring and retention of talented faculty and staff
- changes needed to meet challenges posed by accreditation requirements, maintenance or improvement of student market position, or the institution's mission
- balance between facilities requirements and availability, including both the quantity of space and its suitability for the program activity
- changes in student characteristics (such as preparation levels or the proportion of full-time to part-time students) that require unit adjustments in scheduling, workload assignments, or resource consumption
- balance between availability of course offerings or services and demand for them
- opportunities to enhance revenues or other resources from clients and external sources
- opportunities to improve the use of existing resources and any associated short-term investments required to capitalize on those opportunities

The collection and analysis of information, in short, calls for a comprehensive review of the program unit's operation and the degree to which it is fulfilling its missions. Although much of the analysis entails adding up the need for resources, it must also include thorough study of the means by which a unit can redirect its own resources and acquire additional revenues from sources outside the university; this is necessary if later negotiation attempts are to be effective and credible to the institution's central administration.

Linking Planning and Budgeting

The process of analyzing needs and opportunities and translating them into financial management plans assumes that the institution and its units are engaged actively in planning for both the immediate and the long-term future. In reality, effective planning is often difficult to achieve in an academic setting because of historical and cultural aspects of higher education organizations. Some have claimed that the term "college or university planning" itself is an oxymoron.

Through the history of higher education in Europe and the United States runs a thread of scholarly independence that remains a hallmark of much of today's academic life. The independence of the individual scholar in pursuit of knowledge was maintained in large measure even as groups of learned teachers banded together centuries ago in Europe to share facilities and students and to seek financial support from wealthy patrons, the church, and governments. Although driven by economic necessity to be in the world, academics clearly have fought to avoid becoming of it. Though debates of scholarly issues within an academic discipline can be heated at times, most faculty members maintain an attitude of respect and deference to the interests of colleagues within an institution.

With the concept of collegial governance firmly guiding decision-making processes in most institutions, and an atmosphere of reluctance to do anything that may adversely affect the efforts of other scholars, colleges and universities have been notably conservative in the management of their internal affairs. Some critics over the years have characterized certain academic departments and institutions as afflicted with a "terminal politeness" leading to near paralysis in the face of challenges from a changing world. Others have noted the irony of an institution that often challenges the broader society to reexamine its basic premises and policies being itself the model of conservatism in its internal affairs. Few can quarrel, however, with the remarkable durability of higher education institutions. Kerr (1968, p. 300) cites a long tradition of conservative behavior: "Galileo within the conservative institution of Padua in his day, Erasmus at Oxford and Freiburg and Newton at Cambridge helped start the enormous metamorphosis from which the modern world emerged. But their institutions, as institutions, were stolidly changeless."

Indeed, planning in colleges and universities, as in other nonprofit organizations, is often a zero-sum game because opportunities for major resource infusions are rare. Thus, new initiatives or expanded efforts in some areas must often be undertaken in concert with reductions in others. This means, of course, that the interests of some members of the academic community are likely to be adversely affected. As one faculty member stated: "It is more fun to plan than to be planned."

The former chair of a university academic senate states the problem succinctly (Foster, 1987, p. 5): "Being with a covey of administrators in pursuit of some shining goal—'educational equity,' or 'excellence' or 'outreach,' for example—can be an invigorating experience. Ideas and optimism abound, the sky is (so long as the meeting lasts) the limit. When the product of such sessions ultimately hits the floor of the Academic Senate, the atmosphere may be quite different—suspicious, cynical, sometimes just plain reactionary. The faculty have no stake in change per se; they may feel they have property rights in the status quo."

Researchers in higher education administration have given great attention to the importance of planning in recent years. In particular, strategic planning has been advocated for colleges and universities in the United States. Strategic planning, as opposed to tactical or operational planning, is an active process by which an institution, through the self-discipline imposed by clearly defined phases, combats the normal drift in the strong currents of the status quo and gains control of its own destiny. Much has been written on the subject of strategic planning in higher education; the 1980s have been called the "Age of Strategic Redirection" because of increased focus on external environments and issues of effectiveness, quality, outcomes, and competitive advantage. (See Norris and Poulton, 1987, for an overview of current planning issues and suggested readings.)

A crucial element in strategic planning is a strong, formal link between planning and budgeting to overcome the natural tendency of long-range plans to lie unused on the shelf. A view of the relationship of planning to budgeting developed by McClenney and McClenney (Lisensky, 1987) is shown in Figure 1. McClenney and McClenney partition the development of the financial plan into three overlapping phases: strategic planning, operational planning, and resource allocation. The strategic planning phase combines the review and updating of institutional missions with the assessment of external and internal factors and the development of a strategic plan that serves as the basis for the operational plans created in the process of budget development.

Coleman (1986, p. 58) makes the following observations about the benefits of linking the planning and budgeting processes. "Planning and budgeting are intricately interwoven and have closely related, mutually supporting roles. Planning is an effort to determine and control the destiny of an institution. . . . Budgeting is the pricing or costing mechanism, which develops the financial blueprint for plans. During the repetitive planning cycle reiteration, this pricing or cost mechanism exerts pressure regarding priorities, financial feasibility, and the implementation insights concerning trade-offs and resource commitments and their timing. In the end analysis, planning decisions, like all decisions, must pass the test of judgment and affordability in the absolute sense, as well as in the margin. The end objective is to introduce and manage change toward long-term equilibrium between expected revenue and expenditures." Thus, by forcing the analysis of the financial feasibility of planned actions as early as possible in the planning process, an institution or a program unit becomes unable to avoid facing future realities, as it can with a less detailed planning process.

Facing the future as though it were imminent requires that financial planning have a long-range horizon as well as one covering the immediate future. Most institutions embarking on a

Figure 1. The Model of Strategic Planning by McClenney and McClenney.

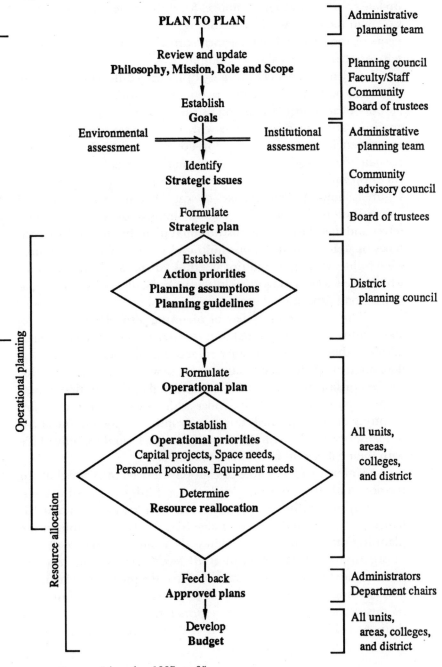

Source: Lisensky, 1987, p. 35.

strategic planning process institute five-year financial plans that are updated annually when the budget for the coming year is prepared. Coleman incorporates the controlling and plan evaluation components of the financial management process into a comprehensive, self-correcting model shown in Figure 2.

Coleman's model for strategic planning differs from standard models as portrayed in Figure 1 in one very significant respect. Most authors treat strategic planning as the domain of the institutional administration in consultation with its program units and other constituencies and refer to it as top-down planning. These authors relegate the strategic plan's implementation—usually termed tactical or operational planning—to the institution's program units. As Figure 2 shows, Coleman makes the case that the program units of an institution also should engage in strategic planning for themselves and that the eventual institutional plan should combine both types of strategic plans. This multilevel view of planning is more compatible with the traditional ethos of academic institutions, which stresses both individual initiative and collegiality or cooperation among professional groups.

This collaborative view of planning also places greater responsibility on the individual units to engage in the financial management that may be necessary to accomplish their objectives. It does not treat the financial planning for new initiatives as the exclusive responsibility of the central institutional administration. Given the near zero-sum conditions under which most higher education planning is accomplished, this responsibility is one that most administrators at the central institutional level would gladly share with their colleagues in the program units.

Unfortunately, a note of caution must be introduced about the potential effects of strategic planning if it is conducted without sensitivity and political judgment. Active efforts to incorporate financial elements and achieve trade-offs as early as possible in the planning process, while they address the common problem of drift in organizational management at all levels, can inhibit creativity and morale if carried out too rigidly. First, the premature classification of programs or activities into winners and losers can have serious negative effects on those sectors targeted for deemphasis or shrinkage. These programs, when visibly sacrificed as part of the trade-off activity of strategic planning, may require special attention if their personnel or constituencies are to adjust to lowered aspirations.

Second, excessively rigid long-range planning may diminish the institution's or unit's ability to accommodate unexpected opportunities and may have a demoralizing effect on the entrepreneurial talents that contribute to the organization's character and attractiveness. To counter this undesirable side effect of planning, it may be wise to establish and adopt formally a strategic goal of positioning the organization to respond to unexpected opportunity and then to develop its operational capability, in the form of identified resources, to meet that strategic goal. Finally, strategic planning, perhaps because of its impressive name, often focuses on broad, dramatic issues—sometimes to the neglect of basic problems in the institution's program units. Planners must always be on guard against falling into the trap of "letting them eat cake." The consequences are predictable if the staff in the trenches have even primitive weapons.

Despite these caveats, however, the benefits of strategic planning are great and many effective higher education leaders instinctively engaged in this type of planning before it acquired its name. At the very least, the long-range plans of institutions and their units should include an assessment of both start-up and continuing costs and revenues from outside sources for new or expanded ventures. These plans should compare future costs with the potential sources of additional outside revenues so that the residual amount of revenue that must be recaptured from internal sources can be determined and used as a target for planned reallocations. The organization should construct a schedule for phasing in the new initiative and recapturing the necessary internal resources. The identification of activities whose support will be reduced can then be timed to meet the internal circumstances of the organization. In some cases it is wise to delay this targeting, for example, when a reprieve may be possible through the future identification of alternative revenue sources. In other cases, early identification can reduce the generalized anxiety that may be created when it is common knowledge that the financial ax will fall, but its target is in doubt.

Figure 2. The Coleman Converging Model of Planning.

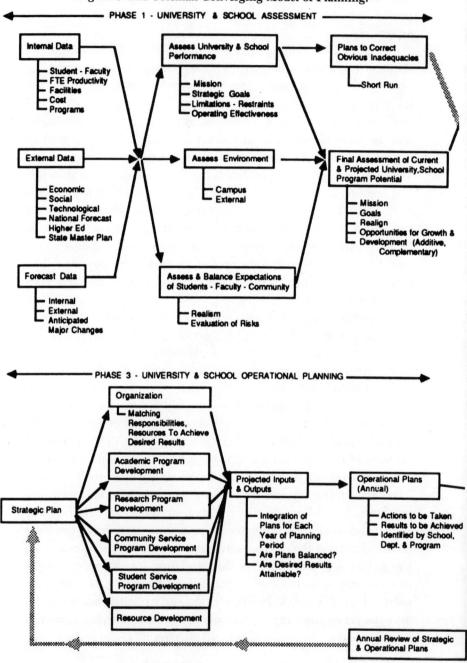

Source: Coleman, 1986, p. 56.

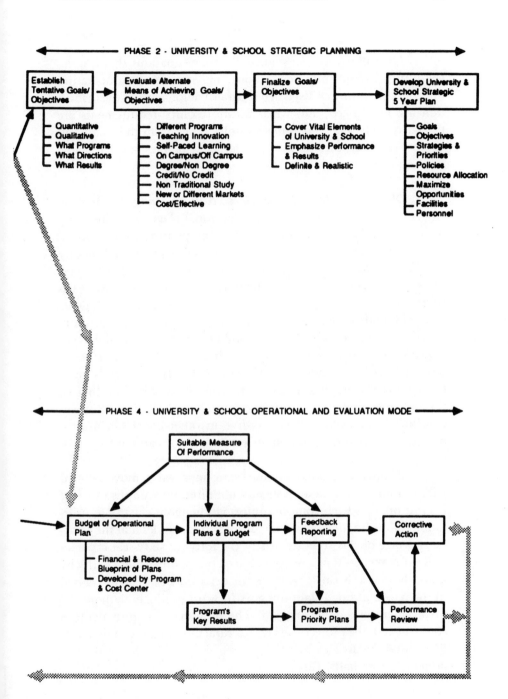

Case Studies

The following case studies illustrate situations that can develop in program units, institutions, and systems when operating units lack planning skills, when separate components of the institution are not linked, and when future resource requirements are not adequately analyzed. The examples range from the small and simple to the complex, but the basic principles are the same throughout.

Old Man Budget, He Just Keeps Rolling Along. The university is bursting at the seams, and additional classrooms are badly needed. At the same time, the faculty is complaining about a gradual increase in section sizes and its effects on instructional quality and faculty workloads. Courses that once contained from twenty-five to thirty students now hold between forty and fifty. Thus, each course section now requires more faculty time for advising students and grading their work; meanwhile, students have less opportunity to participate in class discussions and are given less writing experience through papers and essay examinations. Many departments have proposed that student experiences and faculty workloads could be improved through a more diverse mix of section sizes, that is, through the combination of some large lectures with a return to enrollments of twenty to twenty-five in other courses. Unfortunately, there are not enough large lecture halls on campus to permit this.

Meanwhile, having obtained state approval to move forward with planning for a new classroom building, the campus office of institutional research compiles information about classroom utilization for the financial planning office and concludes that the greatest shortage of classrooms exists in the forty- to sixty-seat capacity range, the very section size range forced on an unwilling faculty by space shortages. Because no academic departments are to be housed in the new building, planning goes forward routinely without the involvement of any department. The program of requirements is completed for the project and architectural drawings are undertaken that contain many classrooms of the size despised by the faculty but no new lecture halls. Changes are made eventually in the plans to include several lecture halls but at the price of additional costs and delay.

Moving On Up. A campus that has always had a strong regional demand among students interested in its music and music education programs has recently achieved a growing reputation in regions of the state it has not customarily served. As a result, applications for admission have increased markedly for the upcoming fall semester and campus officials are pleased that their admissions process can become even more selective than in the past.

When enrollment figures are established for the fall term, however, the campus discovers it has experienced a drop in enrollment and has fallen short of the budgeted target agreed on with state officials. How could this happen? The explanation is surprisingly simple and the unexpected shortfall could have been easily avoided. The admissions office has not adjusted its historical freshman yield rates from offers of admission to reflect the characteristics of its potential new student market. Closer analysis indicates that the college is now competing for students with a number of well-respected institutions, and it is often the back-up choice for many of its applicants. Therefore, it often loses the competition.

A sadder but wiser campus administration does not make the same mistake again. However, it takes the campus several years to convince its system administration and state officials that it is not losing its ability to attract students.

No Program Is an Island. After years of struggling to develop its school of business, a small urban university is encouraged by increased enrollments in business programs. After three years of sustained growth, institutional administrators provide funds for additional faculty and support staff for the school. Suddenly, the bottom falls out—admissions plummet and the percentage of students continuing from one year to the next drops sharply.

A few miles down the road, a large urban university is celebrating the removal of probationary status for its business programs. Having restricted enrollments for more than three years to achieve the lower student-faculty ratio required by its professional accrediting organization, the school of business is once again accepting a large proportion of its applicants for admission. Its enrollments have actually grown only by 20 percent—but that is about the total size of some small programs, for example, the little program up the road.

Creeping Socialism. A private university agrees with the request of its financial aid officer to increase the base budget for financial aid awards by 4 percent more than the rate of inflation. The intent is to make the university more competitive with peer institutions for students with strong qualifications.

In preparation for the second year, the financial aid officer announces that an additional 4 percent augmentation of financial aid awards will be necessary. Their curiosity aroused, staff in the university's budget office review the details of the augmented financial aid program. They discover that the financial aid office has embarked on a major, externally publicized program that increases awards to incoming freshmen by 12 percent above inflation and has used the 4 percent budget increase to fund the program for the first year. To continue it into the second year, of course, the university must provide funding at the higher levels for freshmen and sophomores. At maturity in four years, the program costs are destined to be increased by the full 12 percent provided to each entering class. Because the university is publicly committed to the highly successful program, budget staff must scurry about to find revenues to cover it.

Gift Horse Number One. A member of the university board makes an offer that is difficult to refuse. He pledges a total of $7.5 million to help renovate a large building owned by the university and to advance one of the university's schools in which he has a particular interest. This renovation would convert a useless relic into a usable facility that is badly needed. The total cost of renovation is estimated at $13-15 million; the balance of $5.5-7.5 million is to come from the projected income of a capital fund drive that will use the $7.5 million gift as the anchor to encourage other donors. The $7.5 million is to be paid in ten annual installments of $750,000. Construction is to begin as soon as architectural plans can be completed.

The university's fiscal officer suggests reluctantly that further analyses be conducted before the champagne is uncorked. Indeed, a review reveals that the conditions of the pledge present a difficult challenge for the university. The phased payment of the pledge requires that the university borrow money for construction, at a cost of approximately 10 percent annual interest. Given these conditions, the university could borrow only $4.5 million if it were to pay interest and amortize the debt using the $750,000 annual payment of the pledge. Further, the project, when completed, would entail an additional $200,000 in annual maintenance costs for the augmented space, costs that could not be met by revenues from program growth. Building an endowment of $2 million to cover these additional maintenance costs would be necessary if the university did not divert funds from other programs. Therefore, the university could undertake a $2.5 million renovation effort immediately if it did not use or acquire other sources of income.

Fiscal reality having entered the planning process, the university works out, with the donor's agreement, a program of phased renovation based on an annual assessment of total funds available from the original pledge, other capital drive income, and the diversion of funds from other activities and services. The necessary negotiating process with the donor is sensitive and successful.

Gift Horse Number Two. The dean of an agricultural school is a tireless campaigner throughout the state on behalf of the university and its agricultural programs. People respond to his inspirational speeches and private entreaties with numerous property donations in addition to cash or cash equivalents—farm buildings, grain elevators, farmland, tractors and trucks, cattle, pigs, sheep, and horses. The sheer number of acquisitions at times overloads the central staff's ability to maintain up-to-date inventories of university buildings and landholdings that are scattered throughout the state.

At each year's budget negotiations, the dean points out to the academic and financial vice presidents the rapid escalation of costs for supplies and equipment maintenance for operating the school's programs. Indeed, the school's expenditures for these items is consuming an ever-increasing portion of the available funds, reducing the funds available for support staff to manage ever-increasing holdings of land, animals, and equipment. In most years, the dean is advised that the university has confidence in his ability to manage his major enterprise without significant additional support from the university's general funds.

When queried about the possibility of reducing the agricultural school's supply of land and animals, the dean merely shrugs: "I don't really want us to own all the land in the state—just those nice farms that adjoin ours." The university's financial vice president lies awake many nights counting not only sheep but legions of horses quietly munching hay and oats purchased from the few remaining farmers in the state whose land has not been taken over by the university.

Partially Built Cathedrals. A public arts and sciences college, part of a large state system, is designated in the early 1960s to develop into a graduate research university. After working their way through some internal differences over the new direction, the institution's faculty and administration work diligently during the ensuing twelve years to fulfill that mission. Aided by favorable funding levels and growth related to an excellent undergraduate reputation, doctoral programs are created in several of the arts and sciences, and professional schools are established to complement undergraduate programs of high quality.

Two factors conspire, however, to thwart the campus's progress toward attaining status as a major graduate university. The first is the imposition of limits on undergraduate enrollment by the system administration. The system administration is attempting to protect enrollment levels at less attractive institutions, thereby obtaining better utilization of system facilities and reducing the need for capital expansion. The campus, which had an enrollment base of 2,500 students when its change in mission occurred, has been allowed to grow only to 6,500 students and is held to long-range targets of 9,500 students. The second factor is a two-year fiscal crisis brought on by an economic decline that has reduced the state's revenues.

During the budget reduction studies of the second year, the

campus administration reviews its ability to support the large number of doctoral programs, some small and struggling, that it created. It notes that the strong pressure for resources is related in large measure to those programs and their planned development. In order to calculate the number of faculty required to offer these programs, each department is analyzed to determine the minimum number of faculty necessary to provide subdiscipline coverage for the existing and projected doctoral programs, as well as the enrollment and workload levels necessary for efficient operation given the critical, or minimum, faculty base. The total campus enrollment level necessary to operate the planned programs at realistic student-faculty ratios is then calculated and compared with existing and projected enrollments.

The department of geology, for example, would require a minimum of sixteen faculty members to cover the subject matter range of its planned doctoral programs. The university assumes a feasible student-faculty ratio of 12:1 for this program, a level it could tolerate if the university as a whole were supported at 15:1. To maintain a 12:1 ratio for sixteen faculty positions, it is estimated that the department's enrollment must grow to 192 full-time-equivalent students. If the department continues its current share of university course enrollments, the university will need a total enrollment of 14,000 to reach the break-even point in this department—that is, the point at which reasonable workload requirements justify sixteen positions.

After compiling the results of similar calculations for all departments, the university estimates that its total enrollment must reach approximately 15,000 students if all planned programs are to be adequately staffed by faculty carrying reasonable workloads. This total differs significantly from the target of 9,500 set by the system administration.

The documentation of the large gap between its programs' reach and the university's reasonable grasp shows a reduction in doctoral mission to be the only way to ensure long-range viability. Doctoral programs in some disciplines are reluctantly abandoned and the number of doctoral specialties in several other disciplines is reduced. These actions narrow the gulf between aspiration and achievement and create some flexibility for the institution in meeting its immediate fiscal problems. In addition, the system administration becomes convinced that a moderate upward revision of campus enrollment limits would be in the best interests of the system. Had an analysis linking program plans to future budgetary realities been conducted earlier, all concerned would have been saved much anguish and wasted effort.

Three

Developing
a Realistic Budget
and Financial Plan

❖❖❖❖❖❖❖❖❖❖❖❖❖❖❖❖❖❖❖❖❖❖❖❖❖❖❖❖❖❖

The second phase of financial management of an institution consists of the creation of a financial plan for a designated period of time, customarily one year. The centerpiece of this plan is the institutional budget. The budget is described in NACUBO's *College and University Business Administration* (1982, p. 314) thus: "Institutional budgeting is the process whereby the plans of an institution are translated into an itemized, authorized, and systematic plan of operation, expressed in dollars, for a given period. Budgets are the blueprints for the orderly execution of program plans; they serve as control mechanisms to match anticipated and actual revenues and expenditures."

Two types of budgets are maintained by colleges and universities. The current funds, or operating, budget contains planned revenues and ongoing expenditures to support institutional activities. The capital budget defines estimated resources and expenditures to cover major, one-time acquisitions or projects such as building construction, major repairs or renovations, land acquisition, and major items of equipment. This chapter focuses on the current funds budget, which is developed with the participation of nearly all academic administrators.

The Institution-Wide Budget

The institutional current funds budget is, in fact, a consolidated statement of the separate budgets of all of its units and must therefore be presented in a format that identifies the multiple types of revenue sources and their intended uses.

Table 1 presents the current funds budget summary for the main campus of a large state university in a format that separates both expenditures and revenues into categories that reflect the degree of restriction placed on their use, either by their funding sources or by internal administrative policy. As noted in Chapter One, institutions and their program units may gain their operating revenues from appropriations by government entities, charges to clients for services, gifts, grants, and contracts from external sources, and the investment of institutional resources such as endowments or cash balances. Within each category of income, the funds received may either be available for pooling into an unrestricted general fund or designated for the use of specified projects or program units. For example, the university represented in Table 1 operates with an administrative policy—typical of many institutions—that each program unit retains the earnings that it generates by providing services to clients outside the university. Therefore, revenues gained from such activities are budgeted separately for each unit and then aggregated in column 2 of Table 1 under the category of *designated* resources. These resources are excluded from the pool of *unrestricted general funds* of the university, which are shown in column 1 of both the revenue and expenditure displays.

How Resources Are Acquired. Panel A of Table 1 shows that the university will receive both unrestricted and restricted appropriations from its state government ($145.144 million in unrestricted and $28.866 million in restricted funds). The unrestricted funds are appropriated in the form of instructional subsidies for general institutional support. The restricted funds are provided to support specific programs receiving priority in the state, such as agricultural

Table 1. Budgeted Income and Expenditures of the Main Campus of a Public University.

A. Composition of Fiscal Year Income (in millions)

Sources	Unrestricted (1)	Designated		Total (4)
		Earnings Operations (2)	Restricted (3)	
Government appropriations				
State	145.144		28.866	174.010
Federal	11.097		56.574	67.671
County	1.138		7.174	8.312
Subtotal	157.379		92.614	249.993
Student fees				
Instructional and general	67.265			67.265
Room and board		19.900		19.900
Other		3.997		3.997
Subtotal	67.265	23.897		91.162
Other income				
Auxiliary sales and charges	.018	121.733		121.751
Department and univ. services	.460	14.914		15.374
Endowment income	1.075		3.706	4.781
Gifts and grants	1.645	.180	18.728	20.553
Temporary investments	7.500			7.500
Subtotal	10.698	136.827	22.434	169.959
Regional campus services	1.210			1.210
Total	236.552	160.724	115.048	512.324

B. Proposed Campus Expenditures (in millions)

Expenses	Unrestricted General Budget (1)	Designated		Total (4)
		Earnings Operations (2)	Restricted (3)	
Instruction and general	226.815	14.050	16.270	257.135
Sponsored research	1.171	.838	44.975	46.984
Public service	2.178	93.340	49.135	144.653
Scholarships and fellowships	3.496		3.523	7.019
Auxiliaries	2.693	51.415	1.145	55.253
Total	236.353	159.643	115.048	511.044

services to the public and designated research centers and projects. The university also receives funds from the federal government, the major share of which ($56.574 million) are awarded for specific services and projects and thus are recorded for budgeting purposes as restricted funds.

Most of the income to be received from students comes in the form of instructional and general fees ($67.265 million) and charges for room and board ($19.900 million). The instructional and general fees, which are to be used for the general support of the institution, are classified as unrestricted resources. However, the income from room and board charges is to be used exclusively by the auxiliary organization responsible for operating the residence halls; it is therefore segregated under the category of *designated: earnings operations*. The income thus designated for residence halls is not restricted further; it may be pooled for general operational use within the program unit—that is, within the auxiliary organization that operates the residence halls.

Similarly, nearly all of the income from auxiliary sales and charges ($121.733 of $121.751 million) is designated for use by the units that generate it through charges for services to students or the public. The university hospital and the athletic department are major enterprises in this category. Income from departmental and university services ($15.374 million), primarily from income-producing services provided by the academic departments and schools, is also largely segregated for use by the units that generate it. Small amounts of revenue are excepted from this segregation; this is revenue generated by a few programs that are funded by the university's unrestricted fund and that partially reimburse the general fund with the income they generate.

Endowment income, the return from investment of the various university endowments, and gifts and grants from nongovernmental sources are both largely restricted by their donors or granting agencies. Although these funds must be classified as restricted at the central institutional level, in some cases the uses designated by the donors would otherwise have been supported by allocations from the institution's unrestricted general fund. Under these circumstances the program unit's budget may well show an informal combining of some restricted funds with unrestricted funds in the plan for completing its educational mission.

The $7.5 million expected from temporary investments reflects the fact that the university is in a favorable cash-flow position—that is, it tends to receive its payments before it provides services, compensates faculty and staff, and pays for the goods and services it receives from outside vendors. This institution pools all of its liquid assets for investment and places the resulting earnings with its unrestricted funds; it does not allocate income shares back to those program units generating income from earnings or other sources. In some institutions, particularly those charging overhead or franchise fees to their earning units, this category of income is shared with program units on the basis of formulas that reflect volume and cash-flow factors.

Finally, this main university campus acquires some revenue from charges to the university's regional campuses for administrative services that it provides in such areas as purchasing, personnel administration, accounting.

Although institutions differ in the amount of funds they receive from various sources, this university's basic revenue categories are typical of institutions of higher education. It should be noted that although this is a state university, its revenues are not limited to those provided by its state government; indeed, only 34 percent of its total revenues are provided by that source. Further, in its central institutional budget, revenues are classified according to restrictions placed on their use either by outside funding sources or by internal policies designed to create incentives for active management of program units that are expected to support their activities, wholly or in part, with revenues gained by charging clients for their services. Finally, the practical implication of the classification of a set of budgeted funds as *designated* or *restricted* depends on the organizational level making the classification. In some instances, classifying revenues as designated means only that the institution must reserve them for the use of a given program unit. The unit's budget may therefore treat those funds as part of a pool that can be used for its general operation.

How Resources Are Spent. The categories of expenditures presented in Panel B of Table 1 were developed by the institution to show to its constituencies the distribution of its expenditures across broad program categories. Thus, some expenditure categories cut across organizational structures; in other words, a given program unit's budget may be divided among several of these categories. For example, portions of the planned expenditures for an academic department may be components of the aggregated totals for instruction and general, sponsored research, public service, and scholarships and fellowships. Because a major purpose of an institutional budget summary is to communicate the scope of the institution's activities and priorities to its constituents, colleges and universities often spend considerable thought on developing budget formats that serve their unique environments.

The category of *unrestricted general budget* (column 1 of Panel B), which comprises the funds that the institution allocates to its program units, constitutes less than 50 percent of the total institutional budget ($236.353 of a total $511.044 million). This is primarily because the institution is engaged in a number of research and public service activities in addition to providing instruction to its students, activities that are supported by resources of their own. Institutions vary greatly in the ratio of unrestricted to total expenditures; this ratio depends not only on the breadth of an institution's mission but also on the extent to which its revenues depend on private gifts and endowments, most of which contain restrictions on their use. As this table shows, a college or university can be a complex assemblage of related economic communities. It follows that the financial management of such an institution involves far more than the control and allocation of unrestricted resources to program units.

The major portion of this university's unrestricted general budget ($226.815 of 236.353 million) is used to support instruction and general activities. These activities include departmental instruction and research, libraries, other academic support, sponsored programs administration, student services, plant operation, and institutional support (the university's administration). Allocations of unrestricted funds to other program categories are usually made on a case-by-case basis. For example, an allocation to sponsored research may be made as a matching, or in-kind, expenditure to obtain a research grant or contract. This university also provides significant general fund support to operate television and radio stations serving its community; that support is included in the public service category. Additionally, although the institution's auxiliaries are generally self-supporting, general funds are used selectively to reimburse auxiliary operations providing instructional services; the athletic department, for example, provides some coaching staff and facilities maintenance for instruction in physical education courses. Similar arrangements are also made with the residence halls and university union for staff contributions to the instructional programs.

The Program Unit Budget

The budgets of the program units describe planned income and expenditures in greater detail, using the same basic funding categories as the institution-wide budget summary. For these budgets, it is necessary to specify all of the separate sources of revenue and expenditures for each project carried out in the department and to further segregate planned expenditures into the categories that are used by the institution in controlling the budget plan during the fiscal year (for example, personnel, equipment, operating expenses, and travel).

For those units in the instruction and general category of Table 1, many expenditures are often treated as central institutional costs and are not listed in the unit's budget; examples are costs associated with facilities provision, utilities, and centrally provided services such as the library or computer. The latter services are often allocated to units by the central facility, frequently in terms of goods or direct services rather than dollars. Most auxiliary operations, on the other hand, include such costs in their unit budgets; in fact, those costs may play a significant part in the development of the unit's financial plans.

Table 2 presents the annual budget summary for a typical academic department to illustrate the manner in which the separate budgets for several related, revenue-generating activities can be combined into a comprehensive fiscal plan. Each of the eight

Table 2. Budget for a Theater Department.

	Unrestricted		Designated	A. Revenues		Restricted			
	(1) General Fund $1,292,500	(2) Gifts/ Endowments $54,000	(3) Performances Workshops $541,000	(4) Gifts/Endowments A $63,000	(5) B $102,000	(6) A $97,500	(7) Grants/Contracts B $163,400	(8) C $40,100	Total $2,353,500
B. Total Expenditures									
Faculty (positions)	$ 750,000 (15.0)		$100,000 (2.0)		$ 75,000 (1.0)	$ 27,000 (0.5)	$ 53,000 (1.0)	$12,000 (0.2)	$ 825,000 (16.0)
Staff (positions)	120,000 (4.0)		62,000 (1.5)	$21,000 (0.5)	26,000 (1.0)	40,000 (1.0)	52,000 (1.5)	12,000 (0.5)	184,000 (6.0)
Grad. assts. (positions)	200,000 (20.0)		50,000 (5.0)		20,000 (2.0)	30,000 (3.0)	40,000 (4.0)	10,000 (1.0)	250,000 (25.0)
Supplies/ Services	143,500	21,000	151,000	35,000	5,000	7,000	10,000	2,500	224,500
Travel	2,500	21,000	27,000	7,000	3,000	5,000	3,000	1,200	41,700
Equipment	27,000	12,000	34,000			8,500	5,400	2,400	60,100
In-Kind	49,500								
Total	$1,292,500	$54,000	$424,000	$63,000	$131,500	$117,500	$163,400	$40,100	$2,286,000
Balance	-0-	-0-	$117,000	-0-	$(29,500)	$(20,000)	-0-	-0-	
C. General Use Expenditures									
Faculty (positions)	$ 750,000 (15.0)				$ 75,000 (1.0)				
Staff (positions)	120,000 (4.0)				26,000 (1.0)	20,000 (0.5)	18,000 (0.5)		
Grad. assts. (positions)	200,000 (20.0)		50,000 (5.0)						
Supplies/ Services	143,500	21,000	54,000		5,000		1,000		
Travel	2,500	21,000	6,000		3,000	5,000	3,000	1,200	
Equipment	27,000	12,000	7,000			8,500	3,200	2,400	
Total	$1,243,000	$54,000	$117,000	-0-	$109,000	$ 33,500	$ 25,200	$ 3,600	$1,585,300
Unrestricted General Funds									(1,292,500)
Net Gain for General Use									$ 292,800

columns in Table 2 provides revenue and expenditure information for a set of activities that has its own revenue sources and requires revenue-consuming services that are to be provided by the department. These activities are classified into unrestricted, designated-earnings, and designated-restricted categories. Panel A shows the revenues generated by each activity or category, such as restricted and unrestricted gifts, grants, and performances. Panel B shows the total expenditures for each resource the department uses, such as faculty, supplies, and travel. Panel C shows budgeted expenditures for the general use of the department, derived by pooling unrestricted general funds and unrestricted gifts with funds freed from designated and restricted fund activities.

Generally, activities that augment the unrestricted general budgets for general departmental use do so in two ways: through the overlap of purposes between unrestricted and restricted activities, and through an excess of revenues over expenses in those earnings activities for which charges are made to external clients.

Column 1. The unrestricted general fund allocation to the department of theater and its associated expenditure plan are shown in Column 1. Like most academic departments, its major expense is the compensation of its faculty and staff. The department considers its expenditures for equipment and travel to be very small; this is also common in higher education, where the provision of funds for classroom instructors usually is accorded a higher priority than allocations for equipment or support for the travel of faculty to professional meetings. Obtaining funds for these purposes and to provide financial support for graduate students, who assist faculty in their scholarly efforts, is thus given high priority by the department in its efforts to supplement the institution's general fund support from its earnings and restricted fund activities.

The department has also budgeted expenditures of $49,500 from its unrestricted funds allocation to provide in-kind, or matching, contributions required by the outside providers of funding for two restricted funds projects. The department regards these contributions as an investment to obtain larger amounts of funds to support high-priority activities.

Column 2. The department anticipates receiving $54,000 in unrestricted gifts and income from endowments that contain no restrictions on their use. As with most academic fund-raising efforts, this amount is considerably less than the amount in the restricted category (columns 4 and 5). The department will use these unrestricted funds for expenditure categories considered to be underfunded by the unrestricted general fund: supplies and services, travel, and equipment.

Column 3. Revenues and planned expenditures are displayed in column 3 for a very active program of performances and workshops maintained by the department to provide educational experiences for its students and services to its surrounding community. The performances, which include appearances by noted artists, generate major revenues from the sale of tickets in the community. Joint products of these performances occur in the form of workshops held for students by the visiting artists.

The performances budget shows an excess of revenues over expenditures of $117,000. This will be applied in general use expenditures (Panel C) to provide additional support for graduate assistant stipends and other underfunded categories. Part of this excess revenue is generated by restricted funding in the amount of $63,000 donated by an area manufacturing company for a distinguished artist series (Column 4A) named in the company's honor. Since these funds offset some expenses of the performance program, the restricted funds can be used indirectly to support general use expenditures.

Column 4. This gift, as noted above, provides funding to pay for the public performances of noted artists and the provision of "master classes" or workshops for the students in the theater department. The gift, in which expenditures match revenues, offsets costs that would otherwise be borne by the department's performance program; it therefore contributes indirectly to the department's instructional program.

Column 5. A wealthy patron has provided funds for an endowment to establish a faculty chair in the department. Income from the endowment ($102,000) covers the cost of the faculty member's salary and staff and other support for the professor's programs. As a provision of the endowment, the department matches a portion of the donor's gift. In return for these matching funds ($29,500), the department gains the services of a distinguished professor for its instructional and research programs at a lower cost than the appointment of a junior faculty member would entail.

Columns 6, 7, and 8. Three grants or contracts awarded faculty in the department enrich the department's scholarly activity. Although these awards require that the faculty be released from some instructional responsibilities in the department, they simultaneously provide much-needed graduate assistant stipends and augment department funds for travel and equipment that will be useful to the department for its general instructional program. In the case of Grant A, the department was required to provide an in-kind contribution of $20,000 from its general funds, an expenditure that the department regarded as worth making to acquire $33,500 that augments its core programs.

As Panel C of Table 2 shows, the department has pieced together a set of activities that augments its basic unrestricted general funds allocation of $1,292,500 by $292,800. These activities thereby support necessary activities that are of relatively low priority in the institution's expenditure program for its unrestricted funds.

Because of the joint-product nature of the department's activities, the department has also gained other program benefits that are difficult to quantify. For example, the released time provided faculty with sponsored grants and contracts results in an addition of 1.7 full-time-equivalent faculty on a temporary basis to bring fresh perspectives to the department's programs. The educational program has been enriched by the existence of master classes conducted by visiting artists as well as by the full-time presence of an endowed distinguished professor whose high salary and support costs could not be borne easily from unrestricted general funds.

This example of a specimen department demonstrates the manner in which resources are pooled from multiple sources despite restrictions that accompany specific program activities. A more complete display would have included the more detailed breakdown of expenditure categories found on most higher education campuses, such as the subdivision of supplies and services into such elements as telephone, postage, duplicating, and so on. The reader will have little difficulty making the adjustment to the real-world budgeting environment of his or her institution.

Developing the Financial Plan

Creating a financial plan for the coming year (year X+1) usually requires several months. Agreements should be reached on several features, particularly the number of faculty positions, as early as possible to allow for productive recruitment. In public institutions, a major budget effort is often triggered by the presentation of the state's executive, or governor's, budget to the legislature in early or mid January. This timing allows for better estimates of potential state appropriations to the institution for the coming year. Some institutions, therefore, use the spring budgeting process for year X+1 as the occasion to prepare the institutional request to state officials for the year after that (year X+2).

Whatever the process or schedule used in preparing the financial plan, the plan's objectives must be to provide adequate resources to programs and services for the immediate future and preserve them for the long term. The following discussion is therefore concerned with both the process of creating the financial plan and the characteristics of effective financial management plans. In the creation of the plan, all relevant information, from both institution-wide and departmental or unit perspectives, must be reviewed; strategies and alternatives must be established; and responsibilities for the generation of income and the provision of services must be assigned. In practice, a number of steps are required to attain those goals.

Reviewing and Integrating Information. The information gathered by several offices on factors affecting the institution's plan must be collected, usually in the office of the chief financial officer, and translated into assumptions about costs and revenue potential.

Alternative courses of action, each containing expenditure and revenue projections, are then developed for review by appropriate officers and constituency groups, customarily faculty and student representatives.

Consulting and Reaching Decisions on Key Factors of the Plan. Working with the simulated alternatives, the institution's president or another senior administrator designated by the president usually seeks consultation from a variety of sources about the effects of possible actions and the probabilities that targets for revenue or services can be achieved. The alternatives considered at this stage are usually institutional in scope and reflect what are sometimes termed the strategic elements of the institution's plan. For example, changes in tuition levels and general plans for compensation levels of faculty and staff are considered at this stage. Special initiatives—such as the replacement of instructional equipment, library automation, preventive maintenance enhancement, or the introduction of new programs—also receive attention so that major priorities and strategies can be established with due consideration of their likely financial impact. From this review, the president or chancellor acquires the information necessary to establish the key elements of the guidelines that will be issued to units for the preparation of their more specific plans.

Preparing Plans for the Units. The schools, departments, offices, and other units receive instructions to prepare their individual plans based on the guidelines defined for the institution and on factors unique to their operations. It is at this stage that the top-down planning converges with the planning of the individual departments and administrative units. The guidelines issued to the units contain some general constraints on expenditures from institutional general funds as well as indications of anticipated service and revenue levels. They may also include a provision for units to present requests for special funding to undertake new services or remedy existing problems. The unit must then consider its total revenue potential from all sources and its service commitments and integrate this information into a plan that will be reviewed and approved at the institutional level.

Reviewing and Negotiating the Unit Plans. The negotiation of the elements of the final plan for the units customarily retraces the administrative steps involved in the creation of guidelines. Thus, at the academic department level, the directors or coordinators of programs within the department present plans to the department chairperson. The chairperson integrates these plans into a departmental plan and enters into discussions with the dean. The dean then prepares a school or college plan and undertakes a discussion with the academic vice president. The academic vice president and vice presidents in such areas as student services and personnel present integrated plans for their operations to the president or designated senior administrator. The financial vice president then reviews the plans from all vice presidential areas and provides a critique of them to the individual vice presidents. In some instances, modifications agreeable to both parties are made and a joint recommendation for acceptance is sent to the president. In other instances, a vice president's request may be sent to the president accompanied either by a negative review from the financial vice president or by several alternatives, usually including trade-offs, prepared by the financial vice president.

The roles of the academic and financial officers in this process differ from institution to institution. In some institutions, the chief academic officer also serves as the provost or executive vice president and thus oversees the entire budgeting process. The chief fiscal officer then serves as staff to that officer in the budget process. In other institutions, an executive vice president has oversight of the other vice presidents and the academic officer is one of several vice presidents submitting plans; the financial officers provide staff support for that effort. In most institutions, however, the president presides more or less directly over the process with the financial officer serving as the coordinator. Whatever the process, the negotiations should result in decisions for each unit about revenues available from various sources, revenue production, and levels of service to be provided. These decisions should be formally recorded and made part of the formal financial management plan.

Adopting the Financial Plan. The president customarily presents a final plan to the governing board for its approval before implementing it. Before the plan is adopted by the board, a final consultation with the institution's various constituencies customarily centers on features of the plan that have changed as a result of negotiations with the separate units.

Budgeting Techniques and Tools

A basic challenge facing the administrator is that of translating program aspirations and demands for services into a set of numbers—dollar amounts—that are the foundation of the organization's financial plan. Some numbers, of course, are determined by forces outside the administrator's control. The administrator cannot control inflation or interest rates and lacks the authority to establish allocation levels from the institution, the state, or other funding sources. Market conditions affect enrollment levels and the charges that are made for tuition and other services. The range of costs is narrowed by such factors as traditional demand for services and expenses that must be met to keep programs going—journal subscriptions, clerical assistance, equipment maintenance, and the like.

Nevertheless, the effective administrator searches for ways to gain more control over revenues and costs, seeking tools for making allocation decisions and for projecting revenues and costs under differing conditions. Several techniques have been advanced in recent years to address both concerns. *College and University Business Administration* (National Association of College and University Business Officers, 1982) describes several methods of budgeting that are commonly used by higher education institutions. Among the techniques are incremental/decremental budgeting, program budgeting, zero-based budgeting, and formula budgeting.

Incremental/decremental budgeting is the most widely used approach in higher education. In its purest form, it involves making only limited changes in the organization's revenue levels and distribution of resources from one year to the next. This method receives great criticism from students of management because it embodies a passive approach to administration; however, most experienced administrators know that colleges and universities are relatively stable enterprises whose operation requires long-term commitments of the type recognized by incremental/decremental budgeting. A basic incremental/decremental approach must be accompanied by reviews of workload fluctuations, efficiency, and alternative ways of providing services; these reviews are used to adjust the base budgets of units prior to the incremental/decremental decisions.

Program budgeting—sometimes called planning, programming, and budgeting systems (PPBS)—was introduced into the federal government through the department of defense in the early 1960s in an effort to link planning goals to resource expenditures in complex organizations. In this approach, a program may be carried out by more than one unit or by a single component of a unit. One can well imagine the need for this program-oriented approach to national planning for such elements as potential tactical air support or available ground forces, which are distributed among the branches of the armed services. In higher education, programs may be defined in terms of the undergraduate areas in which student majors are offered. For example, a black studies program may be primarily supported by the history department but may also include offerings from the literature, political science, and music departments. Budgeting then focuses on providing funds to the major department as well as to other departments and offices in proportion to their contributions to the program. With this approach, a department's budget allocation includes a component for each program for which the department provides a supporting role as well as for those for which it has primary responsibility.

During the 1960s and 1970s, this program approach stimulated a flurry of activity at state and national levels in the analysis of academic program costs among disciplines and institutions. However, as Meisinger and Dubeck note (1984, p. 183), "The PPBS concept has generally been more appealing on paper than in practice." The problem, of course, is that the analysis of costs and revenues by program, rather than by basic budgetary unit, is extremely cumbersome when used routinely. Further, many calculations of cost are imputed or inferred rather than directly recorded; for example, one administrator's salary may be distributed among several programs on the basis of assumptions that are subject to debate. Despite its shortcomings, however, analyses of specific activities with program budgeting techniques can provide valuable information for budget decisions when significant actions are being considered.

Zero-based budgeting was introduced as an industrial-strength antidote to the conservatism that is characteristic of incremental/decremental methods. In zero-based budgeting, each organizational unit is required to analyze all costs and justify every element; no budget component is assumed to be part of a continuing budget base. This method is designed to put every category of expenditure on equal footing at the outset, the new along with the established. In reality, however, colleges and universities must make continuing commitments for many of their expenditures if they are to plan effectively and maintain credibility with their constituents. To combat this problem, adaptations of zero-based budgeting have been used, assuming that only a percentage (perhaps 25 percent) of the budget is subject to regular reexamination. Although zero-based budgeting has not gained great acceptance in higher education, many alert program administrators use zero-based techniques for specific problems, usually when costs are escalating rapidly or when significant funding reductions are faced, to determine whether fundamental changes in the provision of services can be made.

Formula budgeting has long been used by higher education institutions and by states to reduce the number of ad hoc decisions to be made and to achieve equity among programs or institutions. In a political environment, agreement on a unit-cost formula to be applied at some future time may well be easier to achieve than agreement on the absolute amount of funding for the coming year. Such formulas also provide some stability for institutional or program unit planning, since they limit the uncertainty about resources to the volume of activity projected and to minor formula changes.

Formulas can be constructed on the basis of average unit costs observed in comparable settings or from models describing how services are to be provided and subjected to cost analysis. Each method has some features that are objectionable to administrators. Formulas based on averages tie funding levels to existing program expenditures and are thus determined in part merely by the funds available in the comparison programs, rather than by actual need. When models are built from basic elements, the funding agent may

well move toward greater control of expenditures at a detailed level
to ensure that the models are a valid representation of needs;
flexibility for program recipients can thus be endangered. Another
significant limitation of most formulas is related to their unit-cost
foundations. The unit-cost measure is a useful general index but it
often does not reflect accurately the marginal cost changes that occur with increases or decreases in volume (see Chapter Six for a
detailed discussion of cost-volume-revenue relationships).

In sum, a variety of budgeting techniques have been advanced over the past few decades, each of which provides a remedy
for a problem facing the administrator. In turn, each is itself accompanied by a set of objectionable features. Seasoned administrators
tend therefore to adopt useful features from each and apply them
selectively to deal with specific situations.

Case Studies

The following case studies illustrate two ways in which an
institution can thwart its own program intentions: through poor
budgetary practices or through lack of clarity and understanding
during the development of the budget. Other case studies concerning the financial planning process appear in Chapter Five.

Starving Academic Programs. A private institution engages
in an annual struggle to keep the wolf from the door. Year after
year, a sense of fiscal crisis pervades the institution. Despite this, the
institution maintains a capital improvements program that ensures
modern facilities—without issuing bonds or otherwise borrowing
against the future, as most United States colleges and universities
do. At the end of each harrowing year, the fiscal officer announces
an unanticipated surplus of income that funds this capital improvements program. The faculty and staff accept the president's thanks
for helping the institution through difficult times and breathe a
sigh of relief.

An analysis of the institution's financial practices reveals the
following:

- Nearly all academic departments operate as "tubs on their own
  bottoms"; that is, income from tuition and other sources is re-

quired to be equal to expenditures, which include an overhead charge for facilities use and institutional administration

- For each department, revenue shortfalls from budgeted levels must be accompanied by matching expenditure reductions during the fiscal year in question
- Unbudgeted revenue surpluses and increases in workload are not accompanied by increased expenditure authorization
- Budget transfers among expenditure categories—for example, from personnel to equipment—are not allowed
- Unexpected revenues from each department revert to the institution at the end of each fiscal year

Some of the institution's internal financial practices motivate the academic departments to generate revenue and maintain tight budget controls. The self-support requirement and the expenditure reductions that accompany revenue shortfalls also provide incentives for revenue production. The inability to transfer funds among expenditure categories can be expected to produce surpluses, given the lack of complete accuracy that characterizes the typical budget process at a detailed level.

On the other hand, one would expect the mandated reversion of revenue surpluses and unexpended funds at the close of the year to provide disincentives for excess revenue production and to promote a tendency to spend up to the budgeted limit. However, in this environment, concern for achieving a balanced budget during the year is dominant; combined with the lack of flexibility in spending funds, it results in the annual reversion of funds from the departments to the institution. Morale appears high among faculty and staff despite the relatively low levels of financial resources available to the academic programs. The leadership of the institution is clearly able to rally people who are committed to the viability of the institution.

However, the quality of the academic programs has been undermined by the diversion of significant levels of current funds to the capital program. In effect, stringent fiscal practices have resulted in actual expenditure levels for academic programs that are lower than thought necessary and planned for during the budgeting process. Thus, high expenditure priorities for capital improvements are an unplanned by-product of a restrictive financial process rather than the result of a considered examination of program aspirations.

Ambiguous Agreement Number One. The student affairs office of a large university has long pressed its case unsuccessfully for the addition of staff for its counseling service. Finally advised in the budgeting process that it should make internal reallocations to fund these positions, the office eliminates its accounting service to student organizations and uses the two positions thus left open to add counseling staff. At a later date, the university budget office notes a $100,000 shortfall in student affairs revenue production. Of course, the revenue drop is attributed to the elimination of the accounting service and the loss of the fees it generates. Restitution is demanded and received.

Ambiguous Agreement Number Two. The computer center, whose charge-back rates to units (based on their use of computer time) have remained unchanged for several years, has grown busier and busier as faculty have begun using the computer more in both instructional and research programs. One by one, the deans have approached the academic vice president for increased allocations to cover deficits in academic department budgets caused by increased computer usage. At the same time, the budget director notes markedly increasing fund balances in the computer center. The director of the center has come forward with a plan for major expansion at no additional cost to the university—that is, without increased general fund allocations directly to the computer center. It is not mentioned that there would necessarily be major increases in allocations to the center's captive clients. A closer look at the rate structure for the center's charges reveals that current rates, set several years ago, were designed to spread the center's major fixed costs among the few users it had at that time. Thus prices are much higher than incremental costs. Since volume has increased greatly, the center is now showing a large profit while academic departments are going broke. The rate structure is adjusted downward, to the dismay of the center's director.

Four

Managing
and Controlling
the Flow of Money

❖❖❖❖❖❖❖❖❖❖❖❖❖❖❖❖❖❖❖❖❖❖❖❖❖❖❖❖❖

In Chapters Two and Three, two of the four categories of financial management activities were discussed: projecting needs and opportunities and creating the financial management plan. Chapter Four provides basic information about managing and controlling the plan and reviewing its viability during the fiscal year. Little has been written on these topics for the academic administrator, perhaps because the typical program administrator is more attracted to the policy activities of planning and budgeting. Nevertheless, program administrators should note that many talented administrators have neglected the details of management and control only to be faced later with fiscal crisis or charges of fiscal mismanagement, at times the result of the activities of subordinates. Many academic administrators lead lives of quiet despair when bogged down by the seeming intransigence of the technical bureaucrats who populate the offices concerned with the control of financial transactions. However, heeding the advice of those technical staff can keep an administrator out of serious trouble.

The academic administrator who understands the basic concepts underlying financial control is in a better position to deal with an environment that may otherwise subvert a plan drawn up carefully to achieve academic objectives. In some ways these aspects of financial management may resemble the detail work of the scholarly life—calibrating instruments, monitoring feeding schedules in the vivarium, checking a primary reference reported in several secondary sources.

Several activities are required to ensure that the conditions of the financial management plan are met and that it can be revised if necessary. These activities are recording and controlling financial transactions, managing the units within the provisions of the plan, collecting and reporting information about the compliance of units with the plan, and conducting regular reviews of the plan's viability.

Recording and Controlling Financial Transactions

The controlling function of financial management may appear mysterious to the academic administrator, who often sees it as an endless series of forms to be signed and periodic reports that are not easily reconciled with his or her records. Indeed, a close examination of accounting and controlling practices sometimes reveals procedures that are unnecessary or counterproductive for effective financial management and merely provide the appearance of control. It is wise to review the institution's control procedures periodically to ensure that they are accomplishing their objectives. This review process can be aided greatly by administrators who understand their objectives and can suggest alternative ways of achieving them.

The controlling functions can be defined broadly as collecting revenue from clients, establishing positions and hiring and terminating staff, making purchases, contracting for goods and services, paying for goods and services, maintaining records of financial transactions, and making budget transfers. Thus, several offices in the institution are simultaneously involved in providing business or administrative services and contributing to the control of the financial management plan. A number of objectives, discussed below, are included in the recording and controlling function.

Ensuring that Budgeted Resources Are Available to Pay for Proposed Purchases or Other Commitments. The simplest type of fund availability check occurs during the purchasing process when a requisition, or request for purchase, triggers a review of the balance in the account to which the purchase would be charged. A positive balance allows the purchase order to be made; the account balance is updated to reflect the additional obligation and lower balance. This review is intended to limit expenditures to the level specified in the financial plan and to provide information regularly to the administrator concerning the level of unexpended resources. Although this institutional check on fund balances is necessary to ensure expenditure control, it does not relieve the administrator of the burden of maintaining current internal records that may include additional agreements for purchases that have not yet reached the purchasing or accounting offices.

Resource availability checks are also made when positions are created or persons are hired. In institutions that have position control procedures, this review determines not only whether sufficient funds are available but also whether the new obligation falls within the number and type of positions authorized by the financial plan. When the transaction involves the transfer of funds into the personnel budget from another budget category, its execution may require the coordinated action of the budget, personnel, and accounting offices. This is not always easily achieved. Integrated information systems are useful in facilitating such transactions when approriate agreements have been reached among the offices.

Ensuring That Authorized Persons Are Making Expenditures. The financial management plan would be quickly undermined if any staff or faculty member could unilaterally commit the institution to an expenditure. The flow of purchase orders and contracts through central offices ensures that the responsible administrators have control over expenditures, accurate information on expenditures is maintained, and vendors are prevented from making unwarranted claims against the institution. Concerning the latter, demonstrated adherence to centralized procedures weakens a vendor's false claim in the event of a dispute over legitimacy.

Preventing Embezzlement, Theft, and Fraud. Nearly every large institution is likely to have instances of embezzlement and theft from time to time. If the incident involves a significant amount of money and attracts public attention, its impact is compounded by a loss of public confidence that can impede the institution's quest for necessary financial support. Presidents and other senior administrators have lost their positions because a staff member, perhaps one barely known to the official, engaged in embezzlement.

The standard techniques to combat such activities employ procedures under which a conspiracy among individuals is necessary for the fraud to occur. For example, reimbursement for travel expenses usually requires proof of expenditure and verification of the work-related nature of the trip by an independent person. Persons handling liquid assets are visually supervised and required to balance the funds recorded with an independent measure of funds received. Persons making payments are required to receive written authorization from a second person who is responsible for both pre- and post-payment reconciliation of records.

At times the procedures to prevent theft and embezzlement can seem cumbersome, and even insulting, to the administrator. However, the results of ignoring them can be much more unpleasant. Such procedures can provide a measure of protection to innocent people who may at some time find it necessary to defend themselves against false accusations.

Ensuring the Appropriateness of Expenditures. The flow of purchase and service agreements through central offices ensures a measure of protection against expenditures made for objects or services that are contrary to institutional policies or do not contribute to its provision of services. Some types of expenditure are obviously inappropriate; most persons would not use institutional funds to buy lottery tickets or personal clothing or to make payments to friends or relatives. Other categories may involve some individual judgment, for example, entertainment expenses, equipment not housed on the campus, first-class hotel accommodations, or travel by spouses who must host receptions or attend other functions. The customary reviews, like those designed to prevent embezzlement, protect both the individual manager from false accusations and the institution from malfeasance.

Verifying the Receipt in Acceptable Form of Goods and Services. The central receiving service of the institution not only provides the convenience of a single port of entry for the vendor; it also provides accountability and quality control, a reliable source for the accrual information necessary to maintain institutional financial records, and a means by which equipment and other inventories can be updated. Decentralized receiving functions place a heavier burden of paperwork on administrators; given individual differences in tolerance for detail, this would probably undermine the reliability of information.

Ensuring the Timely Payment of Vendors and Service Providers. The institution's future dealings with vendors providing necessary goods and services are protected by timely payment practices. Their reliability can best be ensured through a central accounts payable service. The central handling of payments also limits the number of staff members issuing checks, which reduces the risk of embezzlement and fraud. Beyond these factors, however, an experienced accounts payable staff can contribute to financial management through a devotion to meeting deadlines for discounts when they are offered for prompt payment—and by timing payments to obtain the most interest income when vendors are known to be patient about slight delays in payment.

Ensuring That the Institution Receives Favorable Prices and Reliable Quality in the Goods It Purchases. A central purchasing office can sometimes obtain savings for individual units by combining the purchases from several units and buying at volume prices, at times indirectly through purchase contract prices. A central purchasing office often can build expertise in several categories of goods—accumulating price and quality comparisons that would be difficult for a single administrator, with limited experience and a lower volume of purchasing activity, to acquire. At the same time, the central purchasing operation can sometimes be insensitive to an academic department's unique or highly specialized requirements.

For example, in a particular research area a certain instrument may have become accepted as the standard measuring device; using a substitute instrument may well render a research outcome uninterpretable in the existing context. The challenge facing the administrator is to make use of the benefits of a central purchasing office while maintaining an alternate purchasing procedure for exceptional situations that require program expertise.

Ensuring the Prompt Collection of Revenues. Delays in payment by clients not only degrade an institution's cash flow, affecting its ability to meet obligations and lowering the yield from the investment of its assets; they also diminish the prospects of full collection. Therefore, making certain that the institution gets what is coming to it in a timely manner is an important controlling element in its financial management. A central bursar's function has many advantages over one that widely disperses responsibilities for collection throughout the institution. Generally, such responsibilities should be delegated only where incentives for aggressive collection exist, for example, when a unit's expenditure capabilities are tied directly to the cash deposited in appropriate accounts.

It is clear that the skill and fervor with which controlling activities are conducted can significantly affect the institution's short-term and long-range capacity to provide services. Major concerns about reliability and expertise have led to the centralization of many controlling activities. Such centralization carries with it a risk of creating bureaucratic structures and processes that can impede the individual units in the conduct of their business. Therefore, centralized controlling activities must be regularly reviewed and periodically modified to ensure their effectiveness in achieving an appropriate level of control that is responsive to the needs of the academic units. Informed academic administrators are crucial to the maintenance of this balance.

Managing and Reviewing the Current Plan

The established financial plan requires periodic attention throughout the fiscal year to assess its continuing viability and any need for adjustment. The primary responsibilities for managing the plan, however, reside with the heads of the academic and administrative units.

Managing Units. The heads of the many departments and offices of a college or university, operating close to the action, are often the first to discover factors that may affect the viability of the year's plan. Deviations from expected or targeted course enrollments and other measures of volume are often detected at the departmental level before official statistical information can be obtained. Anecdotal information from students can sometimes help diagnose a breakdown in administrative procedures that requires immediate attention. In short, the effective head of a department or office keeps a finger on the pulse, particularly at the beginning and end of an academic term, and alerts the senior officers when unusual events are occurring.

The department head has a particular obligation to ensure that his or her unit is providing its defined services, whether these involve offering adequate numbers of course sections, providing feedback to the registrar about course enrollments, ensuring that faculty supplies are received in a timely manner, or verifying that texts have been ordered and are available to students. It is strongly recommended that the chairperson or director devise checklists of items to be monitored so that important elements are not overlooked. Murphy's Law—whatever can go wrong will go wrong—was not intended to excuse neglect by encouraging fatalism in the face of a mischievous world. Captain Murphy, a development engineer, merely wished to stimulate thoroughness in the review and correction of factors that can undermine an enterprise.

Collecting and Reporting Information. Periodic management reports are essential to administrators at every institutional level. At senior levels, the financial reports must be aggregated so that administrators can gain a global view of income and expenditures, usually with special attention to the extent to which revenue targets are met and the volume of activities occurring in the units—course enrollments, for example—is maintained according to plan. Unexpended balances for the units are usually not given much attention at this level until later in the fiscal year, at which time the senior administrator may be concerned with ensuring full utilization of funds through reallocation when surpluses appear imminent. At the unit level, reports must be in greater detail to avoid overexpenditures or the premature commitment of resources that may preclude later expenditures for items or activities of high priority.

Standard reports on budget status may be issued as often as once a month; these reports usually cover expenditure-budget information. More detailed quarterly reports analyze trends in revenue generation as well as expenditures. At the unit level, a variety of management reports depicting the status of projects or activity assignments may also be useful. It is usually very difficult to design a standard report at a central level that will serve the needs of all units for appropriate information. For example, a unit may customarily face major expenditures during the first or second quarter of a fiscal year for such things as annual insurance premiums or seasonal football expenses or laboratory supplies. In using the quarterly reports to project total-year expenses, therefore, a unit-specific formula based on prior years' monthly or quarterly patterns may be necessary. In most instances, the unit should prepare its own supplementary report series, compatible with the centrally issued reports, that reflects factors that cannot be accommodated in an institution-wide report.

Many academic administrators, faced with institutional reports that are difficult to interpret, are tempted to rely exclusively on internal, perhaps informal, reports. This is risky because the two report series can become irreconcilable over time owing to errors and omissions. As difficult as it may be, a designated person in the unit must have a full understanding of the practices and definitions used in the institutional report series and ensure that the two reports are reconciled regularly. If the task of reconciliation reaches unbearable proportions for many of the units, the centralized reporting practices must be revised.

Reviewing the Plan's Viability. Periodic review of the current year's plan is customarily triggered by operating reports describing the variances between budgeted and actual revenues and expenditures. These reports contain information for a specified period (such as the most recent quarter) the year to date, and the current fiscal year projected on the basis of year-to-date performance. The general reports are accompanied by more detailed analyses for areas in which significant actual-to-budgeted variances are present or projected. When the financial reports are accompanied by reports on workload or volume, they can provide the basis for reallocation decisions among program units or activities within a unit.

These reviews at both unit and institutional levels are essential if the institution is to accommodate potential deficits that result from unanticipated revenue shortfalls or higher-than-expected expenditure levels. Advance knowledge of projected surpluses also allows the institution to move forward on activities that have been temporarily deferred. The purpose of these periodic reviews is, of course, to detect problems before it is too late to correct them and to make calculated adjustments with sufficient lead time to maintain the institution's priorities in the financial management process. The later the decision to make an adjustment in the current budget, the fewer the options that are available.

Case Studies

The following case studies are examples of all-too-common situations in which controlling procedures either were inadequate or were not executed properly. Lest the reader be tempted to scorn the judgment of the people involved or their administrative supervisors, it must be stated that hindsight is always excellent and that all you have to work with in a college or university are people. Caveat emptor.

Embezzlement 101. The foundation of a university has a small-grants program that helps faculty complete scholarly projects or improve aspects of the instructional program. Awards are made for such items as typing a manuscript, traveling to make presentations at international meetings, and hiring student assistants to prepare improved instructional materials. A committee made up of the chairperson of the foundation's board, the foundation's executive director, and the university's academic vice president and financial vice president meets monthly to review applications and make awards. The foundation's fiscal officer serves as staff to the committee; in that capacity, he issues letters of award or rejection and transmits checks to the recipients.

The university's auditor, who is investigating suspected irregularities in the foreign student reimbursement program, engages in a review of check endorsements for checks issued against university accounts. In part because the accounting department is slow in separating the canceled checks of the various auxiliary operations into separate files, she unexpectedly discovers a foundation check issued to and endorsed by a faculty member and signed over for deposit in a personal bank account of the foundation's fiscal officer. This triggers a comprehensive review of the eventual fate of checks issued by the foundation. It is discovered that approximately $50,000 has been embezzled by the foundation's fiscal officer.

The method of embezzlement was simple and risky. The fiscal officer, discovering that no one on the committee reviewed the award and rejection letters, began filing false award letters to rejected applicants and creating unauthorized award checks for them. He then forged faculty endorsements of the checks and deposited them in his personal account. Ironically, the university's academic and financial vice presidents had recently adopted a tough policy on making awards, denying them when they believed other sources of funds were available to faculty applicants for the proposed purposes. This new policy, of course, merely increased the opportunities for embezzlement; the more applications the committee rejected, the more the fiscal officer embezzled.

The financial procedures of the foundation are obviously faulty, relying on the same person to authorize and verify the validity of checks issued. Although the procedures call for two signatures on a check, the second signatory—another staff member in the foundation—must rely on the existence of award letters, created by the first signatory (the embezzler), to verify the authorization of the checks. The problem can be remedied by providing for independent verification of awards and, of course, discharging the foundation's fiscal officer.

The morals: when liquid assets are handled, make certain that a conspiracy will be required for embezzlement; and do not assume that a competent person who works long hours will not steal.

Lines of Credit. The bookstore of a large university, aware of the delays that offices and departments encounter in the processing of requisitions, issues lines of credit to units for the purchase of supplies on an emergency basis. Needless to say, soon all purchases by units become emergency purchases. The bookstore then periodically seeks reimbursement from the university's general fund accounts for amounts owed by the departments and offices.

The results are predictable, of course, to anyone who has had a chastening experience with credit cards. By circumventing the requisition–purchase order route, the units also avoid the review for fund availability that accompanies the standard purchasing procedure. The billings by the bookstore are infrequent, and many units rely on regular budget statements from the accounting office that do not have up-to-date information about bookstore purchases. Generally mystified by the accounting statements, the units do not reconcile internal records of line-of-credit obligations with budget reports. The resulting chaos at the end of each fiscal year leaves many units in a deficit condition, using accrual methods of accounting.

It is impossible to eliminate the lines of credit without disrupting the timely purchase of some items. However, the lines of credit can be tied to encumbrances made by the units to the bookstore in advance of their purchases.

Misleading Controls. University reviews for the availability of funds in the units' budget accounts are conducted at the purchase-order stage; purchase orders are cleared for fund availability and appropriate amounts charged against the accounts when the purchase orders are issued. Often a long period of time elapses between the filing of a requisition, or request to purchase, and the issuance of a purchase order; this results in an accumulation of requisitions awaiting processing. Deans, department chairs, and directors operate with periodic budget statements reflecting fund balances that account only for purchase orders issued.

The result is that many units lose track of encumbrances and annually run out of funds. Purchase orders are rejected or charged against the subsequent year's budget when caught in the change from one fiscal year to the next. The lack of a clear understanding of the type of information contained in the budget reports and the absence of a systematic way to record the potential obligations represented by requisitions causes great acrimony between the accounting office and the units. The university controller believes that any person deemed responsible enough to manage a unit should be able to keep track of outstanding requisitions. In fact, the units need assistance, which is eventually provided.

The Phantom Purchaser. The program director of the campus television station remained in his position for only two years but had a significant impact. The quality of programming improved, as did the size of the station's audience. His departure is followed by the discovery of several unfunded obligations made on behalf of the university.

With wide contacts in the national television industry, the director was able to obtain broadcast rights to many interesting productions on the basis of telephone calls to acquaintances. Materials were shipped to him directly, as were invoices and bills, because suppliers assumed that payments would be forthcoming from the university. After his departure for greener pastures, several of these unpaid bills are found in the files that he left behind for his successor.

It is a prudent practice to instruct any new administrator, no matter how talented, in the procedures for incurring obligations to the university, even when it is assumed that any reasonable person would know that such procedures must surely exist. It is also prudent to question any marked improvements in the quality of services provided by a unit in the absence of comparable improvements in financial support.

Five

Evaluating
and Adjusting
the Plan

❖❖❖❖❖❖❖❖❖❖❖❖❖❖❖❖❖❖❖❖❖❖❖❖❖❖❖❖❖❖❖❖❖

The preceding chapters have dealt with the purposes of financial management, the process of gathering and analyzing information for the financial plan, the basic elements contained in the annual budget, which was identified as the centerpiece of the financial plan, and the control and management of the plan. Chapter Five is concerned with criteria the plan must meet if it is to fulfill the purposes of financial management. Additional concepts will be presented as they become necessary to evaluating the adequacy of the financial management plan: the definition of a balanced budget, accrual recording of financial information, recurring revenues and expenditures, and annual rates of revenues and expenditures.

The terms *financial management plan* and *financial plan* refer to the comprehensive plans that the institution and its program units have created to provide resources in support of services, protect the long-term viability of the institution and its programs, and provide accountability to its constituents. The financial management plan, therefore, contains elements that may not be included in the standard current funds or capital budgets. These elements may include phased plans for the development of programs, agreements

on the specific nature of program delivery methods for which enriched funding has been provided, methods of expenditure control,
and contingency plans in case revenues fall short of or exceed levels
contained in the budget. In short, the financial management plan is
both comprehensive and detailed and covers longer-range features
than are customarily found in an operating budget.

The following criteria for evaluating financial plans contain
specific features that can be classified according to basic financial
management objectives and activities. The criteria are protecting
the asset base, ensuring the provision of resources to activities that
meet organizational priorities, maintaining control as the plan is
executed, and maintaining accountability.

Protecting the Asset Base

Maintain the Organization's Net Asset Base. The plan must
maintain the net asset base, corrected for inflation and the costs of
future activity; that is, it must achieve, at a minimum, a state of
financial equilibrium. As noted earlier, one of the fundamental
purposes of financial management is to preserve the value of
inflation-adjusted assets and avoid future financial obligations for
which revenues have not been identified.

The preservation of assets has its origin in the balanced
budget—in which planned expenditures do not exceed expected revenues—for a specified period of time, usually the upcoming fiscal
year. Although unexpected events and lack of budget controls can
undermine the financial management process, the adoption of a
balanced budget reflects at least the institution's intention to live
within its means.

Most colleges and universities operate with requirements,
either internally or externally imposed, that planned expenditures
and revenues be in balance for each fiscal year. This rudimentary
requirement ensures at least that no obvious debt or reduction in
reserve funds is carried forward from one year to the next. In practice, however, the customary definition, which requires only
explicit balance, allows hidden future obligations to be moved forward and increased over time.

It is recommended, therefore, that the definition of a balanced budget be expanded to include *all* resource consumption attributable to the budgeted period, including the wear and tear on buildings and equipment, inventories of supplies, and baseline compensation levels for faculty and staff that will be carried forward into subequent years. Only with a comprehensive definition of the term *balanced* can the objective of preserving the future-balance between the organization's asset base and its obligations be achieved.

Academic administrators and their funding agencies at times resort to techniques that achieve the appearance of a balanced budget under standard definitions while creating future obligations that may undermine the institution's or its program units' ability to fulfill future missions. Jenny, Hughes, and Devine (1981) present a thorough analysis of these practices in which they compare the educational administrator to the hang-glider pilot waiting for an updraft. The following all-too-common budget-balancing practices are to be avoided:

- Deferring purchases to subsequent budget periods
- Ignoring needs for future equipment replacement
- Deferring building or equipment maintenance when it may lead to major expenditures in later periods
- Building in future budget obligations through partial-year salary or personnel increases

There are times, of course, when the institution or unit may find it necessary to defer expenditures temporarily so that it can continue its services without major disruptions that could affect future student markets or obligations to serve existing student populations. However, these deferrals must be regarded as short-term actions and accompanied by plans to achieve a true balance between resource consumption and acquisition.

Make Reasonable Revenue and Expenditure Projections. The plan's revenue and expenditure projections must be analyzed to ensure a reasonable expectation of attainment. The temptation for the institution or program unit to make optimistic projections of income and conservative expenditure plans is particularly strong during periods of economic hardship. These projections often provide a rationale for postponing difficult decisions to retrench activities, increase charges to consumers, or defer compensation increases for deserving faculty or staff. However, the hard times that make these optimistic projections most appealing are the very conditions under which self-deception can have the most damaging effects on the organization's long-term asset base; an organization can least afford budget projection errors when its resources already are stretched nearly to the breaking point.

Differentiate Recurring and One-Time Obligations and Revenues. The plan must differentiate recurring obligations and revenues from those that are unique to the current fiscal year. Many budgeting systems in higher education do not formally distinguish revenues and expenditures that recur from year to year from those that are one-time or limited in their duration. It is vital that this distinction be made formally if unfunded future obligations or distortions in future annual budget projections are to be identified and avoided. The following situations illustrate the importance of this distinction:

- When start-up costs for a new program or an expansion of services are supported by external funding
- When a significant number of faculty members or other staff are being compensated by grants and contracts
- When a one-time revenue windfall is received
- When an unpredictable revenue source (for example, a state lottery, grant, or contract) is used to fund some activities
- When the institution provides temporary relief to a program unit for what is projected to be a long-term, continuing revenue shortfall or to accommodate gradually to a base budget reduction in general funds allocation

It is recommended that an institution and each of its budgetary units maintain both a current funds budget for each fiscal year and a recurring funds, or base, budget to be used for future years' planning. Both budgets should be kept balanced at all times and any adjustments to the current funds budget for a given fiscal year should be accompanied by appropriate changes in the recurring funds budget. This dual recording of changes is needed to reflect the effect of an immediate decision on the institution's or unit's future and the organization's plan for dealing with revised continuing commitments.

Two general rules are useful in dealing with resources that may fluctuate or have limited duration. First, the duration of an obligation should be matched to the duration of the identified funding; a recurring commitment should not be undertaken without the identification of a recurring revenue source. Thus, when a new venture is undertaken with two- or three-year funding provided by an external source, a commitment to continued operation must be accompanied by an escape clause, and personnel obligations must be made either on a temporary basis or at levels that can be accommodated by the institution or unit through other means, such as normal turnover and reassignment of staff positions from one set of activities to another. An institution or unit should undertake facilities expansion or conversion in response to short-term revenue conditions only if alternative uses of the facilities can be justified separately and accommodated within the institution's or unit's recurring budget base.

Second, resources that are subject to large, unpredictable fluctuations should be used only for one-time or short-term purposes. This practice can diminish pressures by constituencies within and outside the institution to make recurring commitments, such as salary increases that may deprive other institutional programs during future periods in which the fluctuating revenues are low. Several states have adopted lotteries to provide partial support for education, and public institutions have been under strong pressure to use those funds to undertake new programs or increase compensation for faculty and staff. When the novelty of established lottery games wears off and revenues plunge, these recurring obligations create great difficulties for institutions that have succumbed to that pressure. Similar problems have been created by short periods of exceptional market yields from investments. At the very least, the institution's future obligations should be kept at a minimum by matching recurring commitments to extremely conservative estimates of unpredictable revenues.

Base Recurring Budgets on Annual Rate Calculations. The annual rate reflects the costs or revenues associated with an activity if it is carried out over the full fiscal year, the customary budget period. These costs or revenues may deviate significantly from those of a year in which activities are conducted only for a portion of that year. Therefore, when budgeting for recurring expenditures or revenues, it is essential that an annual rate be calculated and used in the base or recurring budget from which future needs and income are predicted.

Several types of action can undermine the control of future expenditure levels in the absence of annual rate adjustments to the recurring or base budget. Among them are mid-year salary increases, the creation of new positions during the fiscal year, and lease or maintenance agreements started late in the fiscal year.

Many state governments and institutions mortgage their futures regularly by funding recurring obligations on a partial-year basis without analyzing the effect that this action has on the budgets of subsequent years. Compensation increases are the category of expenditures most frequently treated in this manner. For example, a 2 percent increase in current funds for a given fiscal year is spent on a 6 percent compensation improvement that is operative only for the last four months of that year. This creates a built-in additional 4 percent increase in the subsequent year's personnel budget, which then has first draw on new funds that may well be needed to meet the inflationary costs of other items. This practice, of course, leads either to a creeping incrementalism in future budgets when funding is plentiful or to the erosion of support for other programs. Such trade-offs are usually not considered fully when the decision to provide an increase is made.

On the other hand, start-up costs for new activities are usually faced before the activities generate income. The first year of operation may incur the costs of a full fiscal year with only partial-year revenues. Subsequent years may well see a closer match between revenues and expenditures, and the institution or unit should take this into account in its financial planning so that future revenues are fully utilized and programs are not unnecessarily or unintentionally subsidized.

Many institutions, lacking a separate recurring or base budget system, have difficulty keeping track of annual rate obligations. The problem is particularly troublesome in large institutions, in which the complexity of budget planning necessarily means that officers and staff at a central level lack detailed knowledge, which can be gained only informally, of the individual components of the units' expenditures and revenues. At a minimum, the budget checklists at an institution lacking a recurring budget statement should include formal reporting by its units whenever annual rate obligations are changed during a fiscal year. To protect the financial status of their individual units, administrators should maintain recurring, annual-rate budgets for their units even if this is not a standard practice in the institution.

Include Venture Capital for High-Priority Initiatives. The long-range vitality of educational enterprises at every level depends on their ability to respond to changing needs and opportunities presented either by market conditions or by improved ways of providing services. Often the required changes involve the investment of current resources to achieve the goals of improved or less costly services, or both.

The specific nature of these initiatives varies markedly in higher education settings. An academic department may provide seed money for a pilot research venture that may not only contribute to the advancement of knowledge but also generate significant income from external sources in the future. The library may invest in new technology that will result in more effective and convenient service and reduce the need for future facilities expansion. The development of new programs may expand an organization's market base or at least protect it from erosion. The retrofitting of existing heating and cooling systems can often result in long-range reductions in recurring utility expenditures long after the initial investment costs have been repaid.

The annual dedication of a portion of the organization's resources to providing venture capital is, of course, necessary to achieve the linkages between planning and budgeting discussed earlier. Some institutions or program units set aside annually a pool of funds whose use is limited to one-time or short-duration projects. The pool is expanded or maintained from year to year by the financial return from projects whose execution has produced recurring savings or revenue enhancement.

Ensuring Resources for High-Priority Activities

Budget Resources to Reflect Consumption Requirements. The immediate problem facing institutional and program administrators in developing an annual budget is ensuring that sufficient resources have been assigned to cover the many activities for which they are responsible. Administrators have an obligation to assure themselves and those to whom they are responsible that all activities undertaken on behalf of the institution are supported currently by resources, allocated to or acquired by program activities, that are adequate to accomplish the established objectives. An organization has a tacit obligation to its clients that it will engage only in activities for which this requirement has been met.

The means of achieving adequate support for programs and activities are few and often difficult to effect. Funds may be reallocated from other activities, additional income may be generated by the institution or the program, the volume of program activity may be reduced, or the program or some of its components may be eliminated. Whatever course of action is chosen, however, the administrators involved must first have the tools available to determine the minimum resource requirements for each activity under their control.

Consider Efficiency Factors and Alternative Means of Providing Services. The goals of this analysis are twofold: to achieve savings that can be reallocated to other activities, and to improve the quality of services. In rare cases, both objectives can be accomplished simultaneously. As suggested in the discussion of the conservative nature of educational organizations, meeting this criterion is difficult as well as potentially beneficial.

Link Planning and Budgeting. The plan must represent the institution's studied response to internal and external factors affecting its operation. For some initiatives receiving priority status in the planning process, venture capital must be invested. In other cases, recurring resources must be devoted in the annual budget to support the planned changes. Because of the press of ongoing activities, new ventures or improvements are seldom on an equal footing with established activities in the competition for scarce resources. As discussed in Chapter Two, one strategy for leveling the playing field somewhat lies in incorporating cost and revenue factors at an early stage in the planning process and establishing an implementation schedule when new, improved, or corrective ventures are to be undertaken. At the very least, these actions place administrators on notice that the necessary resources are to be made available at a specified time through some means—a stronger mandate than one carried by an initiative defined only in general language.

Maintaining Control of Plan Execution

Review Financial Control Procedures to Ensure Effectiveness and Responsiveness to Program Needs. Program administrators typically pay little attention to the mechanisms involved in financial control unless they are stimulated by specific problems such as embezzlement, overexpenditure, or delays in purchasing or hiring. Certainly, when administrators are the clients of services from professional staff, they may generally assume that the institution's chief fiscal officer will be responsible for ensuring that sound practices exist. At the same time, most program administrators must supervise control procedures within their units and have an obligation to assure themselves that their unit procedures provide adequate protection against improper expenditures, violation of budget provisions, and embezzlement or theft. Program administrators must also ensure that effective procedures for reconciling unit and institutional reports are in place. As in most of life's endeavors, some preventive maintenance from time to time can be very valuable in forestalling serious problems.

Define Specific Types and Levels of Services and Review Mechanisms for Units and Programs. The annual budget should contain not only authorization of expenditure levels but also service mandates for the units receiving approval for those expenditures. The financial plan may be viewed as a contract for services. Thus, units' and programs' performance in attaining service levels must be reviewed at appropriate times if the financial plan is to serve as the organization's blueprint for action.

Define Responsibilities for Income Generation and Review Mechanisms. A review of units' performance in the generation of agreed-on amounts of revenue is necessary if the financial plan is to be more than an interesting exercise. In fact, a program or unit's failure to acquire sufficient revenues may compel the administrator to divert funds from other activities to compensate for the shortfall.

Define Effective Review Mechanisms for Central Service Operations. The academic departments and other program units depend on many of the support services operated by the institutional administration for computing services, library acquisition and circulation, reprographics, central stores, and other operations. Because these services usually operate as monopolies, the program units are not free to take their business elsewhere if service is poor or if charges to users are high. Advisory groups representing the program units can monitor these operations' activities to ensure that services are of high quality and that excessive charges are not subverting the intent of the budget allocation process. The financial status of these support operations should be reviewed annually and firm agreements on services and charges should be made during the creation of the institution's annual financial plan.

Make Provision for Regular Review During the Fiscal Year to Determine if Adjustments Are Necessary. These reviews should be conducted at all program levels in the institution. The responsibility for informing the central administration of significant deviations from the current plan should be defined so that the institution can make timely adjustments.

Prepare Contingency Plans for Unpredictable Fluctuations in Revenues and Expenditures. These contingency plans should not only include provisions for revenue shortfalls and unexpected expenditure levels but should also include plans for the effective use of unanticipated excess revenues and savings. The latter provisions will help to ensure that surplus funds are used for items of high priority, not for impulse buying that does not further long-range program goals.

Include Financial Reports Based on Accepted Accounting Standards in Year-End Performance and Status Reviews. Financial statements, to be fully useful, must be based on consistent procedures for recording income and expenses. These statements must then be translated into reports describing the financial health of the institution and its units and the extent to which its actions have been consistent with its own financial plan. In higher education, the standard practice for several years has been to use an accrual accounting system for reporting the receipt of income and the expenditure of funds.

In an accrual accounting system, both income and expenditures are recorded for the date on which the services are actually completed or the goods actually received. Thus, an accrued expense is incurred when a piece of equipment is received and accepted by the institution, or when a consultant delivers a final report. In accrual accounting, therefore, accounts payable and accounts receivable at the close of the fiscal year are treated as expenditure and income charged and credited to that period. This method of accounting differs from the practice of recording financial transactions on the date of payment or the receipt of payment, or on the date when obligations for purchases or services are encumbered or contracted.

A financial statement of fund balances based on accrual practices can be visualized as an index of the net worth of the organization if it were to liquidate its assets, rescind all outstanding purchase orders and contracts, and pay off all its debts as of the date of the report—that is, if it were to go out of business on that date.

Because the institution is continuously providing services and incurring financial obligations, the accrual statement represents an abstraction of, or inexact proxy for, its true financial status. However, even this inexact statement is superior to other means of financial reporting. For example, cash-flow information can be particularly misleading in higher education, where advance payments are often received for services provided over a long period of time, sometimes spanning more than one fiscal year. Under these circumstances, the availability of cash or other liquid assets, in the absence of accrual information, can mask the gradual sinking of an institution or program into desperate financial straits until it is too late to recover. Reliance on cash-flow information can also encourage administrators to deceive themselves and others by making late payments to vendors or others to whom a program is indebted; in short, cash-flow information is subject to manipulation through means not available in accrual systems.

Self-supporting operations—such as auxiliary enterprises, housing operations, bookstores, athletic departments, theater and music performance activities—present particular problems that can be managed only by maintaining accurate records on an accrual basis. A combination of prepayments for season tickets, room deposits, and so on and delayed payments of obligations mandate accrual analyses on a regular basis. An irony in financial management is that these operations, often conducted on an entrepreneurial basis outside the institution's core budget, tend to adhere to accrual practices less strictly than the more stable components of the college or university. This is due in part to the history of many self-supporting activities, which often grow from small beginnings and are thus dealt with more or less informally. The true financial peril faced by many of these operations can also provide a strong motive for self-deception.

Despite its usefulness, the accrual method of accounting has its limitations when used for management purposes. Standard reports must be supplemented or adjusted with other information. For example, the accounts receivable component of accrued income may well overstate eventual revenues and must be discounted in reports if past history suggests intractable collection problems. A strict interpretation of accrued obligations also would treat unredeemed vacation and sick leave as a liability having a real dollar value; in practice, these obligations are usually paid off by a reduction in services when they are redeemed or when personnel depart and are replaced.

Nonetheless, the institution or program that avoids accrual principles in its financial reporting does so at considerable peril and is deprived of a very useful measure of the extent to which its asset base has been protected during the year.

Maintaining Accountability

Procedures for ensuring accountability should include the regular assessment of performance on external grants and contracts as well as the capacity to deliver announced services. By meeting the preceding fifteen criteria, the institution or program unit fulfills most of its obligations for accountability to its constituencies, particularly if it provides relevant information about its activities. In some cases, however, such as when institutional units make agreements with external parties to provide services or conduct projects, there is no mechanism within the university to ensure that agreements have been fulfilled because the agreements have not been made to provide services to the institution. In other cases, the institution may have allowed a unit to announce publicly its ability and willingness to provide professional services to outside clients through institution-based centers.

Because these ventures are undertaken on behalf of the institution, it has an obligation to monitor the extent to which projects are completed and the continuing ability of the unit to provide announced services. To ensure the latter, the institution should annually review activity levels and personnel associated with organized professional-service entities. It should update institutional publications to remove any services that can no longer be provided because of personnel turnover or redirection.

Case Studies

The following case studies illustrate common problems in higher education. In most instances, they are not dramatic; however, they underscore the need for administrators to remain vigilant so that they can prevent or correct such problems.

The Illusion of State Control. A state maintains a cumbersome program of control in its funding of personnel in state universities. This program was instituted after a staff member in the state finance office noted that institutions, in replacing experienced personnel who had retired, often brought in new staff at lower levels and lower salaries. In an effort to prevent institutions from profiting from such turnover, procedures were instituted to control the personnel budgets by providing funds only in the amount actually being paid to staff. Under these procedures, a "snapshot" of the final payroll of a given year (year X) is taken and used as the base budget in preparing the budget for year X+2, adjusted for pay increases already authorized for the intervening year (year X+1). Positions that are vacant in the final payroll period of year X are budgeted for year X+2 near the lower level of the salary range for the position classification on the assumption that such vacancies will be filled with entry-level staff. To compensate for these downward adjustments, the institutions are permitted to reclassify positions, but they are required to provide any differential costs for years X and X+1 by reallocating other university funds.

The tightened procedures have had the effect of gradually but inexorably increasing the personnel expenditures of the universities more rapidly than inflationary pressures would have dictated. The basic distinctions between recurring and one-time funds and between annual rate and current funds have been ignored, with predictable results.

In response to these procedures, the institutions make the following adjustments. First, position vacancies become nearly nonexistent during the last payroll period of the year, even though positions are sometimes filled with temporary personnel. These investments of one-time funds, at less than an annual rate, protect the recurring annual-rate personnel budget from reductions to the bottom of the salary ranges. Second, permanent personnel often are hired late in the fiscal year. Since new salaries at higher levels are covered automatically by the base budget of year X+2, salary offers can be relatively generous. The cost to the university of obtaining a higher-salaried person is a one-time burden for year X+1 and a one-month expense in year X.

Third, retirements are timed to take effect at the beginning of the fiscal year (following the payroll snapshot), thus protecting the salary funding for year X+2. This funding can be used for replacement at a senior level or to generate savings that can be invested on a one-time basis in year X+1 or X+2 to fund other activities. Finally, upward reclassification of personnel tends to occur during the final month of each fiscal year. The institution thus has to fund the salary differential only for thirteen months to receive an automatic funding boost covering the increase on a recurring basis, starting in year X+2. The lowered cost to the institution encourages such reclassifications.

In short, the procedures offer incentives for institutions to invest one-time funds to protect their flexibility in hiring personnel and gain recurring salary increases for their staff. Because state revenues are not inexhaustible, the institutions are inadvertently losing funds for other improvements in programs by using up available resources in this manner. Unfortunately, they are not given the opportunity to make a direct choice and are therefore taking the bird that is in the hand, rather than gambling on the one that may be out there somewhere.

Why Fix the Roof When It Isn't Raining? The director of residence halls, beloved by students, is dedicated to keeping down costs and charges to the residents. Her willingness to tackle even plumbing jobs personally, with the assistance of volunteer helpers, is part of the student folklore. Through ten years of service she has managed to keep increases in room and board rates well below the rate of inflation.

One day late in March, torrential rains sweep across the campus. The director of residence halls telephones the vice president for student services to say that three dormitory buildings have suffered water damage. She asks that several of her students be allowed to move to the campus gymnasium to sleep for a few nights. The vice president goes with a member of physical plant staff to survey the damage and, as expected, finds soaked carpets, walls, draperies, furniture, and student belongings. However, further inspection reveals dry rot in the roof structure and walls and plaster that clearly has been receiving regular soakings for years. A dramatic increase in room rates is made for the following year to repay a loan from the university to replace the roofing shingles on the three buildings, make major structural repairs to the roof and walls on the top floors, replace the top-floor plaster with new wallboard, repaint the interiors of the halls, and replace carpeting, drapery, and furniture.

A budget can be balanced by deferring an interior paint job, but roofs and some other items affect more than fleeting beauty.

A Reversal of Missions. The vice president maintains constant pressure on the bookstore manager to keep prices low to students and faculty, never missing an opportunity to point out to those who will listen that the campus bookstore's prices are much lower than those of a "feather merchant" across the street. Yet many faculty regularly place their textbook orders with the store across the street. The campus bookstore counters with special sales on a variety of items in addition to books to lure faculty back into the fold. Infuriated, the owner of the commercial store requests and obtains a meeting with campus officials. Prepared to defend the rights of the campus store, the campus representatives slowly realize why the faculty are patronizing the other store. In an effort to keep prices low, the campus bookstore refuses to handle orders for texts unless they are bought in quantity. This leaves instructors no alternative for some specialized courses but to place orders with the full-service commercial store. After receiving a full range of services, some are placing all their orders there. It is necessary to state explicitly the bookstore's mission, one that all had assumed was understood without formal definition.

Too Many Birds, Not Enough Roosts. The faculty in the political science department is successful in receiving several grants that have been regularly either renewed or replaced in recent years. Two of its tenured members have been on leave in government service for five years, and the department receives a measure of prestige by their association with it. Faculty members have also been successful in winning one or more sabbatical leaves through the university's program in each of the past four years. Then comes the deluge. The two faculty members on leave lose their government posts because of recent election results and return to campus. Four grants expire without renewal or replacement as sponsored funding in the discipline declines. Because of their past success in the competition for sabbatical awards, none of the productive members of the department are eligible for leave for the coming year. When the department chairperson adds up the totals, there are eighteen funded positions in the department and twenty-two faculty members with claims on positions. The distinction between one-time and recurring obligations and resources is made instantly clear, and the department is forced to swallow its pride and accept the temporary charity of a benevolent dean and vice president.

The vice president tells the department chairperson a story about a man driving a truck down a narrow road. The man stopped frequently to hit the side of the van with a large board, to the consternation of a driver following him. When asked impatiently why he was hitting the truck, the man explained that there was a 2,000-pound load limit and he was transporting 4,000 pounds of live chickens. "I've simply got to keep half of them in the air."

One for the Price of Two. The anesthesiology department of a university's medical school is regarded as a trailblazer in the practice of its craft. With a nationwide shortage of anesthesiologists and increasing demands resulting from new surgical techniques, the department has established "physician extender" practices that make full use of other health professionals. The physical arrangements of the university hospital allow one anesthesiologist to supervise resident physicians and nurse anesthetists administering anesthesia simultaneously in four operating suites. Because complications arising from the administration of anesthesia are rare but require great skill when they occur, this arrangement has allowed for an expansion of surgical services with no increases in mortality rates or other negative effects on the patients served.

During a review of methods for dealing with the practice income of faculty in the clinical departments of the medical school, it is discovered that the anesthesiologists are receiving full payment from third-party payers and individual patients for each surgical procedure they supervise. At the same time, the university hospital is receiving reimbursement for the services of the resident physicians and nurse anesthetists who are employed by the hospital. In short, the patients, directly or indirectly through third-party payers, are being billed twice for a single service.

The solutions, of course, are as simple as they are painful to the physicians. The alternatives are to transfer the residents and nurse anesthetists to the physicians' payrolls as part of their staff and overhead costs, to establish arrangements whereby the physicians reimburse the hospital for these personnel services and the hospital eliminates their cost from the charges to patients and third-party payers, or to use a centralized billing system in the hospital that would eliminate separate billing for physicians' charges, appropriate payments then being made to physicians by the hospital. Following considerable turnover in the anesthesiology department, a system of hospital reimbursement by physicians is adopted as the change bringing the least disruption to all concerned. Accountability to the public is restored.

Serving Two Masters. The athletic booster club at a major university raises a significant amount of money each year to provide the marginal additional revenues considered necessary to bring national prominence to the athletic program. The basic obligations for the support of the program through ticket sales, television revenues, bowl appearances, and student activity fees remain the responsibility of the university. The club's primary focus is on those items that the university would find difficult to justify to its constituents if university funds were used—entertaining press and media representatives, preparing an impressive multimedia show used in recruiting new athletes, providing supplementary travel money so that coaches spending much time on the road are not restricted to state per diem rates, assigning personal cars to selected members of the coaching staff, and providing salary supplements as an inducement to attract successful coaches. These arrangements have grown in volume slowly over time and have been accepted by the university as a means of accomplishing things that would have been impossible for the university on its own.

The results over time are predictable. The funds that are now relied on to run the athletic program at its current big-time level are contingent on the cooperation and goodwill of a small group of supporters who control the fund-raising process. Although the coaches continue to report through university channels to the university president, they report as well to a small group in the community whose legitimacy is not derived from the university's board or elected officials. In the end, the basketball and football coaches find their integrity challenged greatly by pressures from this small group of volunteers for successful seasons. Investigations eventually reveal significant recruiting violations, covert payments to athletes, and irregularities in the athletes' academic records.

The pressures are perhaps most dramatic in intercollegiate athletics, but they exist also in other settings in which a small group of supporters, providing funds that are greatly appreciated initially by institutions, undermine the institutions' control of activities conducted in its name and with its support. For example, many institutions operate radio and television stations with the support of the public. The stations rely on a small group of active supporters, organized usually as a "Friends of" group, who work on fundraising projects. It is not rare for the director of such a station to be more concerned with the direction set by that outside organization than with that set by the university administration, despite the fact that major support may be provided by the university.

These off-line administrative arrangements do not always have undesirable consequences. They do, however, contain the seeds of activities that may leave the university vulnerable to charges that it has not kept faith with the primary constituencies to which it is responsible.

Six

Analyzing Costs
and Revenues
for Reallocation Decisions

❖❖❖❖❖❖❖❖❖❖❖❖❖❖❖❖❖❖❖❖❖❖❖❖❖❖❖❖❖

The college or university administrator is often faced with financial decisions about program direction or scale that can be informed only by appropriate analyses of the costs and revenue levels associated with alternative courses of action. The following questions about costs are typical:

- Can resources be subtracted from a departmental or unit allocation without damaging its programs?
- What prices should be charged to consumers, whether students or members of the outside community, for the services and goods offered by the institution and its program units?
- What resources, if any, should be added to or subtracted from a department or any of its activities in response to changing workload demands?
- What will be the financial impact of initiating or eliminating a program or service?
- What resources will be required to move a program from mediocrity to excellence?

- How can an impending fiscal crisis be averted through savings that will have the least negative impact on the institution's programs or the services provided by its units?
- Within a program unit, are there alternative ways of providing services that will reduce costs or improve quality?
- How can the institution or a unit achieve savings to reallocate resources to activities of high priority?

These questions clearly require a careful analysis of cost-revenue factors, both those being borne or generated currently and those that may result from decisions to modify program volume or other characteristics.

Cost-Income-Volume Relationships

Many academic administrators, particularly those in public institutions, concern themselves primarily with cost factors, such as the amount of institutional support, in reviewing financial options for academic programs. In part, this limited approach can be traced to the nonprofit status of colleges and universities and to the fact that major funding for academic programs and support services may come in the form of a lump sum from governmental sources or pooled tuition income that is allocated among the institution's units. In short, there is often no direct relationship between the amount of income a unit or an activity generates and the resources it consumes. Under these conditions, it is only natural that primary attention is given to determining how best to allocate unrestricted funds, perhaps at the expense of a more sophisticated review of options.

Reviews that are restricted to this limited view of cost analysis can be misleading, however, about the effects of decisions to reduce or increase activity levels. For example, until the late seventies academic institutions and state governments placed great emphasis on unit costs—such as the cost per credit hour or the cost per full-time-equivalent student—of programs and academic departments. Analyses of these unit costs have been used to identify expensive programs; they have also been used as a basis for providing funds to institutions by state governments and to academic departments within institutions, including many private colleges and universities. Unit-cost measures have given rise to funding formulas in which states or other agencies multiply the unit cost (a dollar amount) by a measure of student enrollment to determine resource allocations. Thus, a campus in a formula-funding state might receive the major portion of its state appropriation on the basis of the following equation: $4,000 per full-time-equivalent student multiplied by 12,000 full-time-equivalent students equals $48,000,000.

Although state colleges and universities sometimes complained that the formulas did not recognize adequately the high costs of some mandated programs, most accepted this unit-cost approach during the 1960s and early 1970s, a period of enrollment growth for most institutions. However, as enrollments declined for some institutions in the 1970s—accompanied by proportional reductions in state allocations—the concept of fixed costs, adapted from the private business sector, began to receive serious attention. Educators across the country lamented to state officials that the loss of one student did not reduce the institution's costs by $4,000, or whatever the amount contained in the state's formula. They explained that they had to maintain the same number of course sections to meet the demand created by the remaining students and that facilities and administrative costs likewise were not linked directly to volume, as formulas driven by unit costs assume. (Some state officials with long memories were quick to observe that the institutions did not make that argument during periods of growth, when, the same logic suggests, the addition of students did not require proportional increases in course sections, administrators, or facilities.)

The National Association of College and University Business Officers commissioned a report on the limitations of unit-cost measures by Peat, Marwick, Mitchell, and Company (Robinson, Ray, and Turk, 1977). Entitled "Cost Behavior Analysis for Planning in Higher Education," this report emphasized the role of fixed, variable, and mixed costs in the financial management of higher education enterprises. Despite humorous comments by seasoned fiscal officers about behaving and misbehaving costs, the report of Robinson, Ray, and Turk was followed by other efforts to study the behavior of costs in a variety of higher education settings—for example, in activities as diverse as faculty staffing, physical plant operation and maintenance, student services, and library services. A review of case studies on these topics was published by NACUBO (National Association of College and University Business Officers, 1980).

These studies and analyses make clear the need for administrators to understand the relationships between costs and income at various levels of volume, such as enrollment levels or sales of services and products, for the programs under their control. A reduction in the number of people served by a program can sometimes generate significant savings; in other cases it may be accompanied by disproportionate losses in revenue. Some high-cost programs can grow without increasing the net cost to the institution, even requiring a reduced institutional subsidy; others cannot expand without requiring unacceptable levels of institutional or departmental financial support.

The basic elements determining the effects of decisions to expand or contract program activities are fixed costs, which do not vary directly with volume, and variable costs, which change with volume. The category of mixed costs is useful sometimes in approaching specific problems of costing.

Fixed costs are those expenditures that are the same at low levels of volume as well as at high levels. They customarily include a core set of administrative costs and, in the case of academic programs, the costs associated with maintaining a minimum number of faculty to teach required courses for student majors or provide adequate coverage of specialized topics. Variable costs are those required to supply staff, supplies, and facilities beyond the minimum fixed amount, to handle workload increases related to increases in volume. Mixed costs typically are considered to be related to volume in a stepwise manner, remaining constant over a range of volume changes until a threshold of increase or decrease is reached. For example, new course sections and classes are not added until student enrollments have increased beyond a certain level; at that point, the new sections must be added, even if they are not filled to capacity.

In contrast to cost factors, revenues to support a program, whether obtained directly from clients or through allocation, are often related directly to the volume of activity. The challenge often facing administrators is that of matching revenues that are directly proportional to volume and pricing strategies with costs that are determined by factors in addition to total volume.

Consider the example in which a growing, self-supporting program with a credit-hour enrollment of 1,000 has shown a deficit of $90,000 for the preceding year. An analysis of unit-cost information reveals that the program's unit cost is $240 per credit hour; the maximum competitive fee it can charge students, however, is $150 per credit hour. The administration, wishing to continue the program, decides that the institution can provide only $45,000 of subsidy. Since each credit hour receives a subsidy of $90, the administration tentatively plans to reduce enrollment by 50 percent. However, an analysis of fixed and variable costs reveals relationships of changes in costs to changes in volume that place such a strategy in a new light. These relationships are shown in Table 3.

At current enrollment levels, most of the program's costs are fixed (at $200,000); increases in enrollment actually contribute to the program's fiscal viability. Each unit increase in enrollment generates $150 of revenues and incurs an expenditure of $40, leaving a balance of $110 either to reduce the deficit (at low enrollment levels) or contribute to a program surplus (at high enrollment levels).

This program would break even at an enrollment level of approximately 1,800 credit hours. The planned reduction of enrollment levels from 1,000 to 500 credit hours would not reduce the current deficit; rather, it would increase the deficit from $90,000 to $150,000 because revenues would shrink much more rapidly than expenditures. Although one might search for ways to reduce fixed costs, the gap between revenues and expenditures is so great that it could not be overcome even by draconian measures. Clearly, this program must either outgrow its deficit or be discontinued if the institution is to reduce its subsidy.

The implications for decisions about changes in enrollments or other measures of volume of activity are clear. First, reductions in volume are not always accompanied by proportional cost savings. Second, increases in volume are not always accompanied by pro-

Table 3. Program Cost-Income-Volume Relationships for a Sample Program.

Number of Credit Hours	Fixed Costs	Variable Costs	Total Costs	Unit Costs	Total Revenue	Gain (Loss)
1	$200,000	$40	$200,040	$200,040	$150	$(199,890)
100	200,000	4,000	204,000	2,040	15,000	(189,000)
500	200,000	20,000	220,000	540	75,000	(145,000)
1,000	200,000	40,000	240,000	240	150,000	(90,000)
1,500	200,000	60,000	260,000	173	225,000	(35,000)
2,000	200,000	80,000	280,000	140	300,000	20,000
3,000	200,000	120,000	320,000	107	450,000	130,000
4,000	200,000	160,000	360,000	90	600,000	240,000

portional expenditure increases. Third, reductions in volume can sometimes bring about intolerable decreases in income.

Net Cost-Revenue Relationships

The primary result of an analysis of the fixed, variable, and mixed costs of a program unit or an activity is an understanding of the net relationship of costs to revenues at differing volume levels. This cost-revenue relationship is the financial bottom line that colleges and universities must consider when evaluating potential changes in the scope of their departments' activities, or that a given program unit must consider in reviewing the volume of its activity.

The program unit or institution must achieve a net cost-revenue ratio of one, when all activities are considered, if it is to operate within a balanced budget. However, the separate activities of the institution or department will vary considerably in their bottom-line performance, some having a favorable cost-revenue relationship and others having expenditures that are higher than income. In some institutional offices, such as the development office or the foundation, the ratio of revenues to expenditures is expected to be very favorable, since part of the unit's mission is to offset unfavorable ratios in the academic and support units. Other parts of the institution, such as institutional administration and facilities maintenance, are expected to operate with very unfavorable ratios. Generally, the academic departments as a group are expected to generate revenues (from student fees, governmental appropriations, a share of income from institutional development activities, and other sources) that nearly match their expenditures. In some cases, the income from their activities must also be sufficient to offset at least partially the costs of operating administrative and support units.

For academic departments in particular, therefore, the financial analysis must focus on revenues as well as costs in the consideration of future actions. All revenue factors being equal, academic programs with high unit costs—attributable either to high variable costs or to the combination of high fixed costs and low volume—will have unfavorable net cost-revenue relationships. However, revenue factors are not always equal; some high-unit-cost departments can achieve a favorable cost-revenue status that benefits the remainder of the institution by generating high revenue levels. For example, if state funding formulas recognize a cost differential for high-cost programs, the high-cost department may well produce enough revenues through funding for its enrollment levels to offset its high costs. Some programs and services may attract so much demand that pricing strategies to clients alone can produce favorable bottom-line results. This is often the case in the clinical departments of medical schools, particularly those whose practice activities include surgical techniques for which professional fees are high.

Many institutions are reluctant to attribute in formal reports the generation of income, pooled in the unrestricted general fund, to their separate academic units. Indeed, a formal statement that allows comparisons between imputed income and general fund allocation can strain relationships between the central administration and the deans, between the deans and department chairpersons, and between the department chairpersons and their program directors. After all, approximately half of the units in any institution with a balanced budget will appear to be subsidizing others—in their departments, their schools, or the institution at large.

Nevertheless, the institution or program unit that does not have a clear picture of the net cost-revenue status of its activities can easily make decisions that have unintended negative consequences. For example, an institutional action to decrease enrollments across the board among its units, in response to fiscal constraints, may result in only limited relief because units with favorable cost-revenue relationships are reduced along with those that have unfavorable relationships. Institutions have been known as well to harm their revenue bases by reducing volume in programs with high unit costs in the absence of detailed review that would reveal correspondingly high revenue generation. Cost and revenue factors are inseparable in financial analyses, even when their public linkage requires special efforts to gain the cooperation of the separate administrators.

Reviewing Cost and Revenue Information

Institutions and program units should review cost and revenue information annually to determine if realignment of allocations or revision of revenue and service targets can be beneficial to the organization. Often the academic administrator is looking for savings in the unrestricted general fund that can be reallocated to create venture capital, redress problems in areas of need, or achieve improvements in the quality of selected activities. Of course, a fiscal crisis will also precipitate such a review.

In the search for funds that can be reallocated to activities of high priority or that can generate savings to meet fiscal constraints, the following strategies are customarily explored:

1. Improving the cost-revenue relationships of as many activities as possible through increased efficiency, growth to offset high fixed costs, or pricing strategies to generate higher income levels
2. Achieving growth in activities with favorable cost-revenue relationships
3. Diminishing enrollments or activity levels in activities with unfavorable cost-revenue relationships when these are due to high variable costs that cannot be lowered
4. Eliminating programs or activities with very unfavorable cost-revenue relationships when these are attributable either to a combination of high fixed and variable costs or to high fixed costs and the absence of market conditions that would permit growth

The administrator undertaking a cost-revenue review that may lead to any of these actions customarily examines each alternative for several features: efficiency gain potential, market demand, revenue alternatives, fixed, variable, and mixed cost interactions, the impact of changed activity levels on other programs, and organizational aspirations and goals.

Efficiency. The pertinent questions here are related to the program's current unit-cost status and its potential for correction or change. The following measures aid in understanding the factors underlying deviant unit costs: faculty teaching loads (perhaps measured by weekly faculty contact hours in scheduled classes), course section sizes, and the ratio of student credit hours to weekly student hours in organized instruction. The highest unit costs occur, of course, when faculty teaching loads are low, section sizes are small, and instructional methods require weekly student attendance in formal instruction in excess of the number of credit hours awarded. Very low unit costs, perhaps indicating the need for quality improvements, occur in departments in which faculty teaching loads are high, course sections are large, and student attendance required in formal instruction is low compared to credit hours earned.

The analysis of departments for the correction of costly practices must therefore include an assessment of whether the existing instructional methods are subject to change. With regard to faculty workloads, the issue of opportunity costs—that is, the other activities that must be forgone to achieve higher teaching loads—must be addressed in considering upward adjustments. When faculty workloads are excessive, it is wise to determine whether other activities are being slighted.

Market Demand. It is necessary to understand also whether the enrollment levels in a program are subject to control or whether current levels are a valid measure of the department's drawing power with the institution's student constituencies. In some instances, the efficiency and net cost level of a department can be improved by increased enrollment, either to make better use of its current capacity or to achieve a better balance between its fixed and variable costs and the revenue its activities generate. The absence of market potential beyond existing levels for a program limits the number of options available for dealing with fiscal concerns.

Revenue Alternatives. Decisions about the level of unrestricted fund support for a program or activity should always be accompanied by a review of other revenue sources, existing or potential, available for its support. When a department operates with multiple sources of income from grants and contracts or other services, it may be possible to transfer some expenses to those sources and thus reduce general fund expenditures. In fact, many institutions have found, through reviews precipitated by fiscal crisis, that some revenue-producing activities were inadvertently subsidized by the unrestricted general fund, and they have therefore removed the subsidy. In other cases, a review may reveal that a department or program is not reaching its revenue potential, perhaps because general fund support has been so generous.

When a department or program has a unique pricing structure and market demand is high, it may be productive to increase prices to students or other users to achieve a more favorable net cost level. If these revenue increases are possible, of course, the institution or unit may be able to achieve general fund savings without imposing changes in enrollment levels, faculty workloads, or methods of instruction.

Fixed-Variable Cost Interactions. As noted earlier in this chapter, cost-revenue-volume relationships are crucial factors in determining the effects of decisions to increase or decrease enrollments in a given program. Fixed academic department costs can range from those associated with departmental administration and maintaining a minimum number of faculty to cover subdisciplines to those related to equipment inventories and facilities. For example, a small department with heavy teaching loads and large instructional sections may show disproportionately high unit costs because of its fixed administrative and facilities costs. If variable costs are low and enrollment markets are strong, a strategy of growth may well result in a favorable cost-revenue ratio and improve the fiscal health of the department, school, or institution. On the other hand, enrollment reductions may produce disproportionate increases in unit costs and unacceptable net costs to the institution or other organizational unit.

Impact on Other Programs. The academic programs of an institution exist in a symbiotic relationship with one another; an action taken in one program can affect several other units. Enrollment increases or decreases in physics or engineering programs affect course enrollments in the mathematics department and may well produce unacceptable unit costs or workloads in that department. Thus decisions in a given department or program must be accompanied by an assessment of the effects, favorable or unfavorable, on other departments to ensure that the institution-wide net cost-revenue effects are favorable, or at least acceptable, and that broader program needs are not sacrified.

Organizational Aspirations and Goals. The institution's mission ultimately becomes translated into the expectations that it maintains for each of its academic departments, and the school or department's mission is tied to aspirations for its programs. Therefore, a crucial concern of the review process must be the effect of each fiscal decision on the ability of the institution or program unit to fulfill the role it has assumed or has been assigned by representatives of its constituencies. In the typical college or university, some inefficiencies and unfavorable net cost-revenue relationships must be accepted as a necessary condition of maintaining the integrity of the institution's mission. In some instances, the unit is bound by its mission to maintain a balanced set of program offerings or provide specific services to a valued clientele. In other cases, unfavorable unit-cost levels are borne to reach or maintain excellence in programs of high priority or visibility. Besides their contributions to the mission's integrity, these well-known activities' secondary marketing appeal may more than compensate fiscally for their direct costs to the larger organization.

Making Decisions About Volume and General Fund Support

The program administrator is usually confronted with two types of decisions in reviewing the financial status of academic departments, schools, and programs. These are whether to diminish, maintain, or increase levels of support provided from unrestricted general funds and whether to diminish, maintain, or increase enrollment or other activity levels. These decisions, made on the basis of factors discussed in the preceding section, are directed toward releasing unrestricted general funds for allocation to activities of high priority: correcting problems of low quality or excessive workload, achieving excellence in selected programs, acquiring venture capital for planned activities, serving unmet market demand in some areas, and responding to conditions of fiscal stringency.

The nine options available for these two types of decisions are shown in Table 4. The goals of actions taken—savings, increased revenues, improved quality, and status quo maintenance—are listed for each action, along with the factors to be considered in reaching a decision. Attaining two of the four possible goals of these decisions—achieving savings and increasing revenues in some units—will release unrestricted funds to achieve the third goal, improving quality in others. The fourth goal, maintaining the status quo, may be significant in programs where quality is high or would be threatened by reductions in available unrestricted funds.

Effecting Savings and Generating Income for Reallocation. This section is devoted to the five categories contained in Table 4 of decisions that are made to balance costs and revenues when revenues have been reduced or to improve net cost-revenue status to allow for the reallocation of resources to other programs. Two of the decision categories—to diminish resources and diminish activities, and to diminish resources and maintain activities—focus exclusively on achieving savings. Two—to maintain resources and increase activities, and to increase resources and increase activities—focus on increasing resources. One—to diminish resources and increase activities—is intended both to achieve savings and to increase revenues. In all cases, the ultimate goal is to improve the institution's net cost-revenue status to meet the desired objectives.

Decisions to diminish both resources and activities for a department are usually based on unfavorable cost-revenue relation-

**Table 4. Goals and Factors in Decisions to Change Activity Levels
or General Fund Support in Academic Programs.**

	Diminish activities	*Maintain activities*	*Increase activities*
Diminish resources	Goal: Savings	Goal: Savings	Goal: Savings or revenue increase
	Factors: High, irreversible variable costs Low revenue potential	Factors: High, reversible variable costs Good revenue potential	Factors: High, reversible variable costs Good revenue potential High market demand
Maintain resources	Goal: Improved quality	Goal: Status quo maintenance	Goal: Revenue increase
	Factors: Low variable costs Low market demand Low revenue potential Quality a priority	Factors: Acceptable costs Stable market demand Stable revenues Acceptable quality	Factors: High, reversible fixed or variable costs Strong market demand Good revenue potential
Increase resources	Goal: Improved quality	Goal: Improved quality	Goal: Revenue increase
	Factors: Low variable costs Low market demand Low revenue potential Quality a priority	Factors: Low variable costs or high fixed costs Stable market demand Low revenue potential Quality a priority	Factors: Low variable costs or high fixed costs Strong market demand

ships that are due to expensive methods of instruction that are inherent in the discipline and to nonexistent or limited potential for obtaining additional revenues from external sources. Because these programs have high variable costs, increases in enrollment will not produce lower unit costs. Indeed, enrollment increases in a program with high variable costs will only worsen a cost-revenue deficit. An institution facing fiscal constraints or heavy demands for resources from other units may well decide to cut its losses by reducing enrollments and resources to lower the subsidy required by the department or program. Of course, the most dramatic way of diminishing resources and enrollments is to eliminate the program or unit.

Decisions to diminish resources while maintaining activities are feasible for departments or programs whose high unit costs are associated with high variable costs that can be reduced through gains in efficiency. Savings can be obtained by reducing the number of faculty positions (without undercutting necessary subdiscipline coverage), thereby increasing faculty course assignments, reducing the number of course sections, eliminating unnecessary student contact hours that may have drifted upward because of excess faculty availability, or a combination of these.

Many departments and programs in this category once had high levels of enrollment that have diminished because of market factors or were richly staffed earlier for enrollment growth that has not materialized. In the former case, course offerings have remained at a level appropriate to earlier, higher demand and an underutilized faculty may have emphasized providing more opportunities for students to be involved formally with faculty. In analyzing the correctability of such situations, it must be determined that the opportunity costs of changes—the deterioration of student experience caused by a reduction in contact with the faculty, as well as the increase in faculty workloads—are low enough to be acceptable.

Decisions to diminish resources while increasing activities are feasible for departments that display the inefficiencies of the preceding category to a greater degree and, at the same time, offer programs with higher market demand. Increased enrollment can generate additional revenues that will allow for improved unit costs and a favorable net cost-revenue ratio. Departments in this category may also have the potential to acquire additional revenues through sponsored activities that can offset expenses now borne by the unrestricted general fund.

Maintaining resources and increasing activities can yield acceptable net cost-revenue ratios and unit costs when instructional efficiencies can be gained by increasing teaching loads and section sizes and decreasing the ratio of student contact hours to credit hours. Thus, the departments in this category share most of the characteristics of those in the category targeted for diminished resources and maintenance of enrollment levels. However, the units in this category also have good market potential and thus may achieve a more favorable financial status by filling the existing course sections to capacity and offering additional courses to meet student demand.

High fixed costs may also lead to the selection of a growth strategy to obtain more favorable fixed-variable cost and net cost-revenue relationships. These high fixed costs may be related to the number of core faculty needed for program coverage, specialized equipment and facilities, large instructional support staff, and so on. Whatever the reason, when departments have high fixed costs, it is usually wise to consider allowing them to outgrow their condition.

Decisions to increase resources and activities are appropriate for departments characterized either by low unit costs, favorable net cost-revenue relationships, and high market demand or by high unit costs, low or moderate variable costs, and high market demand. In departments of the first type, the institution is currently using excess revenues generated by the department to subsidize other units with unfavorable net cost-revenue relationships. An increase in both resources and enrollments for such departments represents an investment, capitalizing on high market demand, made to gain additional funds for distribution to other units. This strategy is analogous to that of a business using revenues from sales of its most profitable product to maintain a full product line or to invest in research and development.

For departments of the second type, uninformed critics may well characterize the decision to increase resources as throwing good money after bad. However, the administration must base its decisions on more than the information contained in unit-cost measures, which, after all, are only an indication that an unfavorable financial situation exists and that further study and action are required.

Providing Financial Improvement to Selected Departments. The following three categories of decisions are typically used in providing improvements for departments where quality considerations indicate that such improvements are needed. They involve action to increase resource allocations while maintaining current activity levels, increase allocations while diminishing activity levels, and maintain resource allocations while diminishing activity levels.

Decisions to increase resources and maintain activities are useful for departments marked by heavy teaching loads, large section sizes, low ratios of student contact hours to credit hours, or a combination of the three. At times, an institution's aspirations to quality for a department may be thwarted by the opportunity costs of faculty devoting too much time to formal instructional activities; this can cause them to neglect scholarly or public service activities that should be accorded a higher priority.

Decisions to increase resources and diminish activities are appropriate for departments that have the characteristics of the preceding category, but in greater degree—very heavy teaching loads, extremely large course sections, or unacceptably low hours of student participation in formal course work. These problems can be corrected at existing enrollment levels only by a major infusion of general fund support. If surplus general resources are unavailable and the department is able to limit enrollments without seriously affecting the remainder of the institution, the remedy is to moderately increase institutional support while decreasing student enrollments.

Maintaining resources and diminishing activities is feasible for departments that are differentiated from the preceding two categories by the institution's ability to diminish their enrollments without undue effects on other university programs. Otherwise, these departments demonstrate the same need for quality improvements through their heavy teaching loads, large section sizes, or low student contact hours in course work. The needed improvements can be effected by lowering the enrollment levels to reduce teaching loads and section sizes.

Maintaining the Status Quo. If resource allocations to departments are reviewed regularly, there should be in any year a large number of departments for which corrective actions have been taken in prior years. Thus, several departments should move from one fiscal year to the next with only minor adjustments in resource allocations or enrollments.

Maintaining resources and activities is appropriate for departments that are judged to be operating within acceptable levels on all measures and are not designated for immediate program expansion or improvement. The characteristics of these departments may differ markedly, however, depending on their instructional methods and the missions assigned them by the institution. Their very diversity illustrates the point that resource decisions should be informed, not only by standard quantitative measures, but by policy and mission standards as well.

Case Studies

The following case studies illustrate two sets of problems involving cost-revenue-volume relationships. In the first case, an academic department must increase its course enrollments without a corresponding increase in resources. In the second case, a larger, self-supporting set of programs is on the brink of financial disaster. This case involves a history of practices that ignored most of the concepts presented in this book. For that reason, the author will claim that it is a fictitious case and that any resemblance to actual institutions, existing or extinct, is accidental.

How Much More Can We Take? The history department, among others, has been informed by the university administration that its budget will be corrected for inflationary costs during the next year, but that it must enroll more students to aid the university in increasing its tuition revenues. The administration notes, in particular, that the department has restricted the enrollment levels in its introductory course sections and thereby impeded the progress of students in fulfilling their general education requirements. Using information on the distribution of section sizes in the department, the administration points out that sixty of the eighty sections offered by the department, with class sizes ranging from ten to thirty students, account for only 50 percent of the department's total enrollment of 2,400 students. It is suggested that the department abandon some of its smaller courses and divert those faculty resources to meeting the lower-division demand. As the final straw, the administration also informs the department that its urgent plea for additional graduate teaching assistants must be denied.

The department despairs of meeting the new conditions. The

lower-division courses are already ungainly with an average of sixty students per course, too many for meaningful class discussion or frequent opportunities for writing assignments. Further, an honest assessment would reveal that only six or seven of the department's thirty faculty members are effective at teaching the introductory course. Finally, the faculty are united in their belief that students should have the benefit of experiences in several small courses; they are adamant about protecting the department's practice of maintaining at least 50 percent of its course enrollments in sections of ten to thirty students.

One faculty member notes ruefully that the large sections currently are so unmanageable that "they might as well have 150–200 students in them." Turned on its ear, that statement is taken as the point of departure for the department's eventual strategy. The department converts the twenty sections containing sixty students each into ten large lecture sections of 140 students each, using five of the faculty members who were the most effective teachers. With the resources gained by eliminating ten sections, the teaching loads of those faculty members are reduced by one course each to allow for extra time to prepare and to read student papers. The remaining resources are used to provide five graduate assistants for these courses and to add two more courses that would enroll twenty to thirty students each.

The administration accepts the department's offer to enroll 200 additional students in its introductory course and forty in other courses. No one is entirely pleased with this outcome because it rests on the continuation of large sections in the introductory course. At the same time, however, the actions restrict the assignment of faculty to that course to those who can best deal with it, and they also provide more time and support to those faculty.

Multiple Transgressions. A statewide set of degree programs is operated by a university system on a self-supporting basis from student fee income; start-up funds, gradually diminishing over a three-year period, have been provided by a major foundation. The program features self-paced learning and a variety of individualized instructional methods that entail major fixed costs for development and maintenance.

Enrollments have grown steadily, at approximately 20 percent a year, since the program's inception, and they now exceed 3,500 part-time students. The total program budget is approximately $4.0 million annually.

The fiscal arrangements are complex. Several affiliated institutions across the state provide services and receive reimbursements based on annual budgets that fluctuate with enrollment levels. Having grown rapidly from small beginnings, and lacking the customary immediate controls on expenditures made by the affiliated institutions, the program has operated without financial statements based on a verifiable accrual system. A memo bookkeeping system (based on expenditures and revenues) is maintained because accrual information is difficult to gather from so many sources. Until recently, funds have been available to meet payrolls and payments to participating institutions.

The program director asks the system administration for approximately $135,000 in assistance for the coming fiscal year. Having been advised in the previous year's budget hearing that the program had reserve funds of $250,000, the system's chief academic officer, upon learning that the financial information is not based on accrual accounting, directs a full-scale financial review to be conducted. That study, requiring months to translate existing information into an accrual format, reveals a negative fund balance of approximately $900,000.

A partial reconstruction of the program's financial history demonstrates the importance of accrual accounting and the perils of relying on information based on collections and payments of revenues. Table 5, which presents estimates from a history that cannot be fully reconstructed, shows clearly that a growing deficit was masked for years by a combination of advanced payments by students and late billings by institutions seeking reimbursement.

In year 1, for example, when the program reported a fund balance of $200,000, by accrual methods of accounting it was already in debt by approximately $150,000 owing to advance payments of matriculation fees (to be held in reserve to cover final graduation transcript checks), late billings by institutions providing services, and the normal positive cash flow associated with the collection of course fees prior to the payment of instructors and

Table 5. Comparison of Discrepancies Between Memo-Bookkeeping Financial Statements and Accrual-Method Financial Statements for Three Years.

Year	External support	Fund balances		Reconciliation
		Reported	Accrual	
1	$1,000,000	$200,000	$-150,000	$ 50,000 Advance fees 100,000 Late billing 200,000 Normal positive cash flow
2	750,000	225,000	-400,000	100,000 Advance fees 300,000 Late billing 225,000 Normal positive cash flow
3	500,000	-125,000	-900,000	125,000 Advance fees 400,000 Late billing 250,000 Normal positive cash flow

staff. These factors grew as enrollments increased until the $125,000 cash-flow deficit in year 3 triggered the financial review.

The factors leading to the program's financial crisis were small in number yet deadly in consequence. First, no quantified long-range plan or budget had been constructed to deal with the shrinkage of the start-up foundation funding. The growth of the deficit in years 2 and 3 parallels the decrease in foundation support. One-time funding was used to cover recurring expenses in the absence of a recurring budget containing plans to make up the shortfalls as such funding decreased.

Second, the lack of accrual accounting and a favorable cash flow caused the program administration to be misled by its own financial information. The program would have been better served with no financial information than with the faulty cash-flow information, which, combined with rapid growth, lulled its personnel into a false sense of well-being. Because expenditures were made by other institutions and reimbursed at a later date, the lack of accrual information also led to problems of budget control. These institutions sometimes overspent their budgeted amounts in a given year, but the lack of accrual information, combined with late billings, meant that it was possible for some year 1 obligations to be charged against year 2, and so on, thus masking overexpenditures made by the institutions.

Closing the program altogether was not feasible. It was estimated that the costs of honoring commitments to students already enrolled would approach $2.5 million and would violate agreements with the foundation that provided support for its operation. Interestingly enough, the dominant program offered was very successful; because of its high fixed and low incremental costs associated with increased enrollments, its growth was nearing the point at which it could break even, if it reduced its fixed costs and increased fees moderately. Having demonstrated that it was meeting a very real need, this program was assigned to an existing institution and provided eventually with state support. Other, smaller programs were either phased out or taken over by institutions to reduce fixed overhead costs.

A suggestion to academic administrators taking on new responsibilities: Do not assume that sound financial practices undergird the operations you have inherited, even when they appear to be on solid footing. It is sometimes necessary to ask the elementary question—for example, has this information been recorded on an accrual basis? At worst, this will be insulting to subordinates. Asked at a later date, however, it may be the stimulus that uncovers a disaster in the making.

Seven

Building Competence
in Financial Planning
and Management

❖❖❖❖❖❖❖❖❖❖❖❖❖❖❖❖❖❖❖❖❖❖❖❖❖❖❖❖

The reader, after completing the preceding six chapters, may have additional questions about financial management or may wish to pursue selected topics in greater detail. Chapter Seven provides an overview of some areas of potential interest and directs the reader to sources that provide more detailed information. Finally, this chapter contains some general advice to new administrators.

Using Information Technology

Effective financial management decisions depend in large measure on intelligent use of quantitative information concerning projected activity levels, needs for resources, potential levels of revenue generation, ongoing rates of revenue consumption and generation, and the financial status of the unit or institution.

Fortunately, major advances in computer technology during the 1980s have created useful information tools that are economically feasible to nearly every administrator charged with financial management responsibilities. In many instances, a major portion of information needs can be met by software tailored to the unique institutional or unit environment and used with microcomputers that also serve as word processors for the unit's communications activities. For some purposes, the general-purpose spreadsheet programs available in the commercial market can be used to deal with the matrices of information involved in financial planning.

Early planning tools, developed originally for use with mechanical calculators, took the form of models that simulated students' progress from birth to kindergarten, through high school, and into college. College admission levels were predicted on the basis of the number of young people at a given age level, known as the cohort group, and the percentage of past cohorts that eventually enrolled in college. Colleges and universities used past market shares of incoming students in the relevant population to predict the size of future entering classes.

The same basic cohort methodology was extended to project students' progress through institutional programs and to form total enrollment estimates for the future. As central computers became available, models based on the past course selection patterns of students enrolled in different major programs were introduced in the form of the induced course-load matrix. This was used to predict enrollments in specific disciplines at various instructional levels. At the same time, course enrollment and budget information were combined to analyze program unit costs. The unit-cost information was subsequently used in conjunction with enrollment analyses to estimate future budgetary needs for the academic programs.

With advances in computer chip technology that dramatically increased data handling and calculation capabilities, simulation models have been developed to allow for analysis of the effects of multiple planning options. These options are based on several factors, such as enrollment levels, variations in fees and other revenue sources, inflationary pressures, and changes in levels of services and unit costs.

Hopkins and Massey (1981) provide a comprehensive overview of planning models in higher education, including theoretical aspects and an analysis of the limitations of models in financial planning. Sheehan (1987) provides a review of the current status of information technology in supporting decisions and an annotated bibliography of recent publications on the topic. For information about continuing developments in the use of information technology, publications issued by the following associations are useful: the Association for Institutional Research, CAUSE (an association devoted to information technology), the National Association of College and University Business Officers, and the Society for College and University Planning. Publications issued by the National Center for Higher Education Management Systems and the Jossey-Bass New Directions series, particularly the higher education and institutional research series, often contain useful material on trends in the use of information in higher education administration.

Using Financial Statements

Many program administrators find it necessary to work with formal financial accounting information in addition to budget statements of the type discussed earlier in this book. The four basic categories of financial accounting reports, usually covering one fiscal year, are concerned with revenues, expenditures, fund balances, and changes in fund balances from one year to the next. If prepared according to acceptable practices in American higher education, these statements will be based on the principles of fund accounting and accrual recording of revenues and expenditures discussed earlier in this book. The fund balance statement is regarded as an index to the net worth of the organization and may be of interest to external entities, such as bonding or lending agencies, in assessing its ability to handle debt.

A concise overview of accounting reports using fund accounting methods is contained in *Ratio Analysis in Higher Education* (second edition), published by Peat, Marwick, Mitchell, and Company (1982). The National Association of College and University Business Officers (1987) has released *The Basic Fund Accounting Training Package*—with audio cassettes, slides, student workbooks, and an instructor's manual—to introduce administrators to the concepts and practices of higher education accounting.

Reconciling accounting reports with budget statements is sometimes difficult because of different recording practices. For example, in budget statements, expenses are typically recorded at the purchase-order stage to provide an accurate record of remaining uncommitted funds; in accounting statements, expenses are recorded on an accrual basis, that is, for the date on which goods or services are actually delivered. These recording discrepancies, which are due to practices maintained for specific purposes, can cause some expenses charged to the budget for year X to appear as accrued expenses for year X+1 in accounting reports.

Several recording practices in financial statements have been the subject of controversy in higher education over the years, and many disputes remain unresolved. The information contained in financial reports may occasionally lend itself to misinterpretation even when the organization's reporting practices are considered acceptable by many professional accountants. It is desirable, therefore, that administrators and managers learn enough about these issues to be informed clients of the organization's accounting services. The administrator should pay attention to the following areas when dealing with financial accounting statements.

First, some assets, such as investments or land and facilities, may be recorded on the basis of their original cost rather than their current market or replacement value. Supplementary information is required, therefore, by administrators contemplating decisions involving these holdings and seeking a refined assessment of the status of the organization's assets.

Second, restricted income is customarily recorded in the annual revenue statement only when it is expended. Thus, these statements may not reflect current successes in obtaining restricted assets for the future support of activities when unexpended, and therefore unrecorded, balances are carried over from one year to the next. Likewise, serious declines of restricted awards in a given year may not be reflected until a later financial reporting period, when expenditure levels have been reduced.

Third, until recently, the accepted practice was not to record depreciation of facilities in financial reports. Although the Financial Accounting Standards Board (which has vied for authority over financial reporting in higher education with the Governmental Accounting Standards Board) has ruled that depreciation should be recorded as a liability in financial statements by 1990, many in the accounting profession argue on technical grounds that its inclusion violates the principles of fund accounting. It is sufficient to note here that the administrator will probably require supplementary analyses to address such questions as the magnitude of the organization's future obligation for capital construction and whether current financial plans are adequate to meet that obligation.

Fourth, the definition of restricted funds in accounting statements encompasses only those funds for which legally binding restrictions exist. Thus many types of income that are realistically off limits for general organizational use are classified as unrestricted funds. This category includes income generated for services provided by academic departments or other entities not formally designated as auxiliary enterprises, income that could not be generated if it were not dedicated to the provision of the services for which the charges are made to clients. This accounting definition can lead to an overestimation of available general use funds. It can also be damaging to an institution's or unit's quest for funds from outside sponsors, who may apply a commonsense meaning, rather than a technical one, to the term *unrestricted.*

Finally, obligations carried over from one year to the next for staff vacation and sick leave are customarily not recorded as an expense in higher education financial reports, despite the otherwise general practice of using accrual accounting methods. Normally, those expenses are met without additional cash expenditures and are experienced only as periods of employee absence when they are redeemed. However, during periods of high staff turnover or fiscal constraint involving staff retrenchment, payments for these accrued benefits to former staff can be a burden that previously went unreported as a debt that was built up over prior years.

In short, the administrator must be alert to technical definitions in financial statements that differ from the meanings assumed by the nonprofessional person, as well as the limitations of standard accounting reports for aiding administrative decisions. Leaders in the accounting profession have for some time distinguished between financial accounting, which "is concerned mainly with how accounting can serve external decision makers, such as stockholders, creditors, governmental agencies, and others," and managerial accounting, which "is concerned mainly with how accounting can serve internal decision makers, such as managers" (Horngren, 1977, p. 4).

Although most financial reports in higher education are classified as "financial" rather than "managerial," several authors have developed reporting formats with the intent of increasing the management utility of financial statements. Peat, Marwick, Mitchell, and Company (1982) advance recommendations for using standard report information to create ratios describing institutional financial status. A joint publication of the Association of Governing Boards of Universities and Colleges and the National Association of College and University Business Officers (1979) provides suggestions on combining accounting and other information to assess institutional health. A financial self-assessment workbook (Dickmeyer and Hughes, 1980) is also recommended to readers desiring information on developments in this area. The monthly *Business Officer*, published by NACUBO, provides up-to-date coverage of deliberations on the various accounting issues discussed in this section.

Responding to Fiscal Crisis

Many American colleges and universities, unfortunately, have gained experience in dealing with financial exigency during the past two decades. Both independent and public institutions across the country have suffered significant reductions in resources because of declining enrollments or unanticipated shortages in state revenues. Often, the crisis's occurrence during the academic year makes the institutional response more difficult. Since personnel expenditures constitute 75 to 80 percent of the typical college or university budget, two factors limit the available responses to revenue shortfalls: commitments to enrolled students for academic courses and services and contractual obligations to faculty and staff, obligations that are renewed typically for a year or longer.

Under these conditions, even a small mid-year revenue shortfall can have major significance for nonpersonnel portions of the budget. For example, if nonpersonnel expenditures represent 25 percent of the total budget, a mid-year shortage of 5 percent of the total budget can require a 20 percent cut in the nonpersonnel budget if immediate personnel retrenchments are not possible (.05 divided by .25). If the reductions must be borne solely in the second half of the fiscal year, they can escalate to 40 percent of the uncommitted portion of the nonpersonnel budget. Fortunately, some staff turnover can usually be counted on in a large organization to take a portion of the burden from nonpersonnel items.

Most institutions must deal with stringency in two phases if revenue shortages are expected to extend into subsequent fiscal years. The first phase tends to be opportunistic—that is, focused on unspent current balances; travel, supplies, equipment, library acquisitions, and lower-level staff positions (where turnover is higher) bear a disproportionate share of the reduction. The second phase is usually marked by a more careful assessment of long-range priorities, analyses of means to enhance revenue production, and the generation of plans to reduce personnel and other recurring expenditures.

Generally, institutions have approached long-range fiscal problems by moving progressively from conservative actions, when modest reductions are required, to actions that may significantly alter the institutional mission, when severe shortages are encountered (see Vandament, 1978). Conservative approaches often involve attempts to raise the revenues of core program activities by increasing charges to clients, improving the marketing of services, intensifying development activities, or using grant and contract resources to support some expenditures previously borne by the institution's unrestricted general funds. Another conservative approach is to search for ways to reduce expenditures through increased efficiency, using analyses similar to those discussed in Chapter Six.

In some cases, however, institutions have found it necessary to eliminate entire programs and services, reduce institutional size to adjust to projected long-term revenue decreases, or take bold program initiatives to develop new student markets. Steeples (1986) has documented the actions of eight independent institutions in which new or reaffirmed program missions were instrumental in meeting problems of market demand. The histories of five institutional responses to severe, recurring revenue declines are documented in a NACUBO study entitled *Reallocation: Strategies for Effective Resource Management* (Hyatt, Shulman, and Santiago, 1984). Hyatt, Shulman, and Santiago identify several conditions that shape an institution's response to fiscal stringency: the timing and duration of the fiscal crisis, the institution's state of preparedness, the institution's financial management flexibility, the diversification of revenue sources, the historical level of recurring program support, and the effectiveness of communication with constituent groups. The authors note that many of these factors are the result of organizational efforts that precede the onset of the crisis and, further, that a prudent approach to financial management requires the building of adequate contingency funds, periodic analyses of mission priorities and cost-revenue relationships of programs and activities, the assembly of revenues from multiple sources, and a history of productive consultation with faculty and other constituencies.

For further information on this topic, the reader is referred to the discussion by Meisinger and Dubeck (1984) of retrenchment and reallocation, in which governance and contract issues involved in faculty retrenchment are elaborated. Inventories of specific methods that institutions have used for both short- and long-term fiscal crises are presented by Ginsberg (1982) and Mingle (1982) and summarized by Meisinger and Dubeck (1984). Publications by Frances (1982) and Mingle and Associates (1981) are also useful on the general subject of institutional retrenchment.

Becoming an Effective Program Administrator

Throughout this book the author has advocated an active approach to financial management. This has been done to counter what is perceived to be too often a passive or dependent attitude in higher education administration, an attitude that is more appropriate to street beggars and offspring from moneyed and titled families. An active approach is therefore advocated in scanning the environment for opportunities and threats, in assembling financial resources from multiple sources, in searching for internal trade-offs when resources are not available for new ventures or correcting existing deficiencies, in looking for ways to improve the net income-cost ratios of programs, in administering and controlling the financial plan, and even in questioning the existing financial management procedures when they appear to thwart program aspirations.

Consistent with an active approach, the author has also advocated increased financial management responsibilities and expertise for administrators of the institution's program units, a key group largely ignored in the published literature on financial management. An institution that does not develop the financial skills of unit or department administrators, and does not charge them with major responsibilities in solving at least some of their financial challenges, encourages the evolution of a welfare state in which the units are the wards and the senior administrators become the guardians responsible for solving all financial problems at every institutional level. Therefore, in each activity of financial management, from the assembly of information to the construction of strategic plans and the controlling of the annual budget, this book has stressed the role and the responsibilities of the department or unit administrator.

Efforts have also been made in this book to relate recommended practices, wherever possible, to the basic purposes of financial management stated in Chapter One. The author hopes that the administrator will constantly evaluate local procedures and practices on the basis of their usefulness in meeting those basic purposes. The effective administrator is one who knows when to raise questions about institutionalized financial practices that serve no useful purpose or even impede effective management of resources.

Although many public institutions operate with severe and counterproductive restrictions and procedures imposed by their states, the author is convinced that more institutional flexibility often exists than is used. Further, college and university administrators sometimes only complain about red tape without making proposals to their funding agencies for alternative ways to meet the agency's accountability concerns. College and university administrators themselves sometimes impose needless bureaucratic procedures on the units within the institution.

The academic administrator, who will probably never achieve a high degree of competence in all aspects of financial management, must gain access to the best technical persons available and cultivate productive client-professional relationships with them. If a gulf separates the program and fiscal affairs staff at an institution, it must be bridged if the program unit lacks resources to create its own expertise.

In some cases, this is accomplished by demonstrating a serious interest in effective financial management to staff who are accustomed to having such matters treated lightly by program administrators. In others, the task is one of accommodating to narrowly focused but technically gifted staff who may treat financial management practices as ends in themselves rather than as means to accomplish program goals. At times, helpful expertise can be obtained when the administrator learns enough of the technical concepts to understand a fiscal professional who lacks the ability to communicate with a complete novice.

The administrator must adjust to the multiple roles that are required of academic administrators in the financial management process. The department chairperson is not only a critical analyst of intradepartmental requests for funds or proposals for new initiatives but also must be an effective supplicant and advocate for departmental interests with persons outside the department. Inadequate performance in either role undermines the chairperson's credibility in the other. Chairpersons who pass on departmental requests to deans without making adequate assessments, including searches for internal reallocation or other self-help methods, will soon find that their effectiveness as advocates has eroded. Conversely, a department chairperson whose commitment to advocacy is considered to be weak will find that rigorous analysis of internal requests is met with cynicism, hostility, or (worse yet) despair. Achieving balance between these roles is not sufficient; the chairperson must be actively engaged in both. The same conditions apply to deans, vice presidents, and presidents in dealing with multiple constituencies.

A comprehensive review of higher education governance, management, and leadership by Peterson and Mets (1987) provides an excellent point of entry into the literature on several issues of significance in academic program administration. The administrator will gain much by reading three thoughtful and personal analyses of higher education administration by experienced practitioners. Eble (1978), who reminds us that "the root and body of the word *administer* is *to serve*" (p. 2), describes the tasks of administrators at all levels—from "Exploring the Territory" and "Getting Things Done" to "Keeping Sane" and "Making Decisions"—emphasizing the personal and political nature of the work. Walker (1979), who warns us of the problems that result from "the marriage of power and innocence," (p. xii), uses caricatures of inept administrators to make points about the importance of diplomacy, patience, respect for others, and professional commitment in college and university administration. Adams (1988), who emphasizes the academic department, serves as a cultural anthropologist who guides the reader through a tour of the academic tribes. All three books communicate much about the subjective experiences of academic administrators and can serve as mentors to the administrator facing new responsibilities.

Among the duties of program administration, those of financial management and personnel decisions are often the most difficult. Financial decisions and actions, in the final analysis, have both personal and social effects. They affect the quality of services to people and the personal aspirations of faculty members and professional staff. And they are made by individuals and small groups whose personal characteristics may have a pivotal effect. The tools and techniques covered earlier in this book can often temper the idiosyncracies of individuals, but they will never eliminate them. The wise administrator, therefore, seeks knowledge about the behavior of higher education institutions and their parts, gains an understanding of the cultural and social factors operating in his or her own organization, and is introspective enough to know how his or her personal characteristics interact with the accepted duties.

The case studies have been included not only to illustrate the consequences of ignorance of sound financial practices but also to encourage vigilance and attention to detail in financial operations. Among other things, one must maintain the realistic view that human beings, even those deserving of high regard, can make errors; it is extremely difficult to create processes that will trigger an appropriate response to every eventuality. Reasonable people must, of course, reject the sense of futility encouraged by popular interpretations of Murphy's Law; however, it is prudent to assume that whatever can go wrong will—unless breakdowns in process are prevented through careful preparation and the existence of contingency plans that take into account human frailty as well as uncontrollable acts of nature.

The administrator has an opportunity from time to time to gain great satisfaction from the financial aspects of his or her duties. In fact, money cannot buy the rewards of seeing a program gain strength, avert disaster, or sustain itself under difficult circumstances through creative and effective management.

Glossary of Financial Terms

◆◆◆◆◆◆◆◆◆◆◆◆◆◆◆◆◆◆◆◆◆◆◆◆◆◆◆◆

Accrual-method accounting. Accounting method in which income from and expenditures for services and goods are recorded for the date on which the services are actually performed or the goods actually received.

Annual rate adjustment. A calculation of the costs or revenues that would result from an activity if that activity were carried out for a full fiscal year; used in budgeting for recurring costs or revenues that begin in the middle of a fiscal year.

Balanced budget. A financial plan in which income is equal to or exceeds all resource consumption, including depreciation, and does not defer expenses to future budget periods.

Capital budget. Budget of the estimated resources and expenditures required to support major, one-time acquisitions, construction, or renovation. See also *Current funds (operating) budget* and *Recurring funds budget.*

Cost-income-volume relationships. A calculation showing changes in revenues and costs that are attributed to increases or decreases in the volume of such items as enrollments, numbers of courses or performances, grants, and contracts.

Current funds (operating) budget. Budget of the estimated revenues and expenditures involved in the support of institutional operations for one fiscal year, exclusive of one-time expenditures for capital purposes. See also *Recurring funds budget* and *Capital budget.*

Designated funds. A fund classification that includes restricted funds and those unrestricted funds that have been dedicated for use by the institutional organization generating them.

Fixed costs. The costs of operating a department or program that do not change with variations in the volume of activity.

Formula budgeting. Budgeting method in which a unit-cost measure (such as cost per credit hour) is multiplied by a measure of volume (such as total number of credit hours for which students are enrolled) to determine the amount of funding a program requires. See *Unit costs.*

Fund accounting. The method of recording financial transactions in which separate accounts are maintained for activities based on restrictions or limitations imposed by agencies supplying the funds or by the institution's governing board.

General use budget. A financial plan incorporating unrestricted funds and selected funds from designated or restricted sources that can be used for general operation—that is, a plan showing the total funds available to support the organization's primary missions.

Incremental/decremental budgeting. Budgeting method that uses essentially the same budget from one year to the next, allowing only minor changes in revenue levels and resource distribution.

Induced course-load matrix. The tabular representation of the distribution of course enrollments across the institution's offerings by students sharing a common characteristic, such as student major, gender, class standing, or age.

Joint products. Two or more outcomes resulting from a single effort or activity, such as the supervision of a student thesis that both instructs the student and contributes to the knowledge base in a discipline.

Line-item budget. A financial plan that specifies in detail amounts of money that can be spent for particular items and purposes. Usually accompanied by control procedures to ensure that specifications are not violated.

Net cost-revenue relationship. The net difference between the fixed and variable costs of a program and the revenue it generates.

Operating budget. See *Current funds budget.*

Planning, programming, and budgeting systems (PPBS). See *Program budgeting.*

Program budgeting. Budgeting method in which budgets are created for specific programs or activities, rather than departments, and each program's budget is apportioned among the several departments that contribute to the program's activities.

Recurring funds budget. Budget of the estimated revenues and expenditures for institutional activities that are continued from one year to the next, as well as for obligations that must be borne and revenues that will be used beyond the current fiscal year. See also *Current funds budget; Capital budget.*

Restricted funds. Funds that may be used to support only those activities specified by the donor or funding agency, or only when certain conditions imposed by the donor or funding agency are met. See also *Unrestricted general funds.*

Strategic planning. An approach to planning that stresses comprehensive environmental scanning and explicit organizational decisions on major directions, thus creating the basis for tactical or operational planning.

Tactical (operational) planning. The implementation of the institution's strategic plan, usually by departments or program units.

Unit costs, unit-cost measures. The cost of a fixed unit of a department's or program's activity (such as a credit hour). Unit-cost measures multiply the unit cost of a program by the program's volume of activity (the number of units it provides). See also *Formula budgeting.*

Unrestricted general funds. Funds that may be pooled and used for an institution's general operations. See also *Restricted funds.*

Variable costs. The costs of operating a program that vary with the program's volume of activity. See also *Fixed costs.*

Zero-based budgeting. Budgeting method in which all units are required to justify every expenditure for each year's budget; no component of the budget is considered to be a stable, or recurring, expense.

References

❖❖❖❖❖❖❖❖❖❖❖❖❖❖❖❖❖❖❖❖❖❖❖❖❖❖❖❖❖❖❖

Adams, H. *The Academic Tribes.* (2nd ed.) Urbana and Chicago: University of Illinois Press, 1988.

Association of Governing Boards of Universities and Colleges and National Association of College and University Business Officers. *Financial Responsibilities of Governing Boards of Colleges and Universities.* Washington, D.C.: Association of Governing Boards of Universities and Colleges and National Association of College and University Business Officers, 1979.

Brigham, E. *Fundamentals of Financial Management.* (4th ed.) New York: Dryden Press, 1987.

Coleman, J. W. "Planning and Resource Allocation Management." In H. Hoverland, P. McInturff, and C. E. Tapie Rohm, Jr. (eds.), *Crisis Management in Higher Education.* New Directions for Higher Education, no. 55. San Francisco: Jossey-Bass, 1986.

Dickmeyer, N., and Hughes, K. S. *Financial Self-Assessment: A Workbook for Colleges.* Washington, D.C.: National Association of College and University Business Officers, 1980.

Eble, K. E. *The Art of Administration: A Guide for Academic Administrators.* San Francisco: Jossey-Bass, 1978.

Foster, J. "Campus Culture." *Senate Forum*, 1987, *2*, 2-5.

Frances, C. (ed.). *Successful Responses to Financial Difficulty*. New Directions for Higher Education, no. 38. San Francisco: Jossey-Bass, 1982.

Gardner, M. *The Annotated Alice*. New York: Bramhall House, 1960.

Ginsberg, S. G. "120 Ways to Increase Income and Decrease Expenses." *Business Officer*, 1982, *16* (6), 14-16.

Hopkins, D. S. P., and Massey, W. F. *Planning Models for Colleges and Universities*. Stanford, Calif.: Stanford University Press, 1981.

Horngren, C. T. *Cost Accounting: A Managerial Emphasis*. (4th ed.) Englewood Cliffs, N.J.: Prentice-Hall, 1977.

Hyatt, J. A., and Santiago, A. A. *Financial Management of Colleges and Universities*. Washington, D.C.: National Association of College and University Business Officers, 1986.

Hyatt, J. A., Shulman, C. H., and Santiago, A. A. *Reallocation: Strategies for Effective Resource Management*. Washington, D.C.: National Association of College and University Business Officers, 1984.

Jenny, H. H., Hughes, G. C., and Devine, R. D. *Hang-Gliding, or Looking for an Updraft: A Study of College and University Finance in the 1980's—The Capital Margin*. Wooster, Ohio, and Boulder, Colo.: College of Wooster and John Minter Associates, 1981.

Kerr, C. "Conservatism, Dynamism, and the Changing University." In A. C. Eurich (ed.), *Campus 1980*. New York: Delacorte Press, 1968.

Lisensky, R. *Linking Planning with Budgeting: A Management Seminar*. Boulder, Colo.: National Center for Higher Education Management Services, 1987.

Meisinger, R. J., Jr., and Dubeck, L. W. *College and University Budgeting*. Washington, D.C.: National Association of College and University Business Officers, 1984.

Miles, R. E., Jr. "The Origin and Meaning of Miles's Law." *Public Administration Review*, 1978, *38*, 399-403.

Mingle, J. R. *Redirecting Higher Education in a Time of Budget*

Reduction. Issues in Higher Education, no. 18. Atlanta, Ga.: Southern Regional Education Board, 1982.

Mingle, J. R., and Associates. *Challenges of Retrenchment: Strategies for Consolidating Programs, Cutting Costs, and Reallocating Resources.* San Francisco: Jossey-Bass, 1981.

National Association of College and University Business Officers. *Costing for Policy Analysis.* Washington, D.C.: National Association of College and University Business Officers, 1980.

National Association of College and University Business Officers. *College and University Business Administration.* (4th ed.) Washington, D.C.: National Association of College and University Business Officers, 1982.

National Association of College and University Business Officers. *The Basic Fund Accounting Training Package.* Washington, D.C.: National Association of College and University Business Officers, 1987.

Norris, D. M., and Poulton, N. L. "Institutional Planning, Strategy, and Policy Formulation." In M. W. Peterson and L. A. Mets (eds.), *Key Resources on Higher Education Governance, Management, and Leadership: A Guide to the Literature.* San Francisco: Jossey-Bass, 1987.

Peat, Marwick, Mitchell, and Company. *Ratio Analysis in Higher Education.* (2nd ed.) New York: Peat, Marwick, Mitchell, and Company, 1982.

Peterson, M. W., and Mets, L. A. (eds.). *Key Resources on Higher Education Governance, Management, and Leadership: A Guide to the Literature.* San Francisco: Jossey-Bass, 1987.

Rao, R. K. S. *Financial Management.* New York: Macmillan, 1987.

Robinson, D. D., Ray, H. W., and Turk, F. J. "Cost Behavior Analysis for Planning in Higher Education." *NACUBO Professional File,* 1977, *9* (5), 1–51.

Sheehan, B. S. "Decision Support Systems and Information Technology." In M. W. Peterson and L. A. Mets (eds.), *Key Resources on Higher Education Governance, Management, and Leadership: A Guide to the Literature.* San Francisco: Jossey-Bass, 1987.

Steeples, D. W. (ed.). *Institutional Revival: Case Histories.* New Directions for Higher Education, no. 54. San Francisco: Jossey-Bass, 1986.

Vandament, W. E. "Reordering Priorities and Adjusting to Reduced Revenue." In E. M. Crawford and W. E. Vandament, *Building Stable Support Systems: A Practical Guide.* Washington, D.C.: University Associates, 1978.

Walker, D. E. *The Effective Administrator: A Practical Approach to Problem Solving, Decision Making, and Campus Leadership.* San Francisco: Jossey-Bass, 1979.

Index

Accountability: evaluation of maintaining, 87, 91-92; as fundamental, 9; maintaining, 11-12
Accounting, financial or managerial, 119
Accreditation, and professionalism, 16
Accrual accounting system: and cost analysis, 112-113; for financial reports, 85-87
Activities, organizational, supporting, 10-11
Adams, H., 125
Administrators. *See* Program administrators
Assets: and annual rate calculations, 80-81; in financial statements, 118; net, maintaining, 76-77; protecting and enhancing, 9-10, 76-82; reasonable projections for, 77-78; and recurring and one-time obligations and revenues, 78-80, 90-91; venture capital for, 81-82

Association for Institutional Research, 117
Association of Governing Boards of Universities and Colleges, 120
Auxiliary enterprises: and accrual accounting, 86, 90; designated resources for, 46; and fund accounting, 13; and general funds, 49

Brigham, E., 6
Budgeting: concept of, 43; formula, 59-60; incremental/decremental, 57-58; planning linked with, 28-35, 82-83; program, 58-59; techniques and tools for, 57-60; zero-based, 59
Budgets: balanced, 76-77, 89-90; capital, 43; concept of, 43; of current funds, 78-79; examples of, 45, 50; in financial plan, 43-62; institution-wide, 44-49; operating, 43; for program unit, 49-54; of recurring funds, 78-79, 80-81

135

Cash-flow information, as misleading, 86
CAUSE, 117
Chief financial officer: and financial plan, 54, 56; responsibilities of, 17-19
Coleman, J. W., 30, 32, 34
Computers, uses of, 115-117
Conflict of interest, and faculty role, 16, 20
Contingency plans, for control, 84-85
Control: aspects of, 63-74; background on, 63-64; case studies on, 71-74; centralized, 68; for effectiveness and responsiveness, 83; evaluation of maintaining, 83-87; and financial reports, 85-87; functions of, 64; and managing and reviewing financial plan, 68-71; and recording transactions, 64-68; regular review of, 84
Costs and revenues: analyzed for reallocation decisions, 94-114; background on, 94-95; case studies of, 110-114; information review for, 101-104; net relationships of, 99-101; and volume and general fund support, 104-110; volume related to, 95-99, 110-111. See also Fixed costs; Opportunity costs; Revenues; Unit costs; Variable costs

Decision making: and financial plan, 55; by program administrators, 125; on reallocation, 94-114
Departments. See Program units
Depreciation, in financial statements, 118-119
Devine, R. D., 77
Dickmeyer, N., 120
Dubeck, L. W., 21, 58, 122

Eble, K. E., 124
Efficiency: and cost analysis, 102, 107; evaluation of, 82; role of, 8-9, 11

Embezzlement, preventing, 66, 71-73
Erasmus, D., 29
Europe, higher education history in, 17, 28-29
Evaluation: of accountability, 87, 91-92; aspects of, 75-93; of asset base protection, 76-82; background on, 75-76; case studies of, 87-93; of control, 83-87; of resource availability, 82-83
Expenditures: appropriateness of, 66-67; authorized persons for, 65, 74

Faculty: professionalism, 16; responsibilities of, 20-21
Financial Accounting Standards Board, 118
Financial management: activities in, 2-3; aspects of, 1-22; case studies of, 21-22; competence in, 115-126; concept of, 7; control in, 63-74; cost analysis in, 94-114; evaluation of plan in, 75-93; financial plan for, 43-62; financial statements for, 117-120; and fiscal crisis, 120-122; higher education factors in, 12-16; information technology for, 115-117; procedures and policies in, 7-8; projections in, 23-42; purposes of, 5-12; responsibilities for, 16-21; scope of, 1-5; task of, 5; terms in, 127-129; views of, 3, 6
Financial plan: adopting, 56-57; aspects of, 43-62; background on, 43-44; and budgeting techniques and tools, 57-60; case studies of, 60-62; concept of, 75; and control, 68-71; and decision making, 55; developing, 54-57; evaluation of, 75-93; information review and integration for, 54-55; institutional and unit, 55; and institution-wide budget, 44-49; objectives of, 54; program unit budget in, 49-54; projections for, 23-42; reviewing and negotiat-

ing, 56; role of, 5; viability review for, 70-71

Financial reports and statements: and control, 85-87; and financial management, 117-120

Fiscal crisis, responding to, 120-122

Fixed costs: concept of, 97; relationships of, 98-99; and variable costs, 103-104, 108

Foster, J., 29

Frances, C., 122

Fund accounting, in higher education management, 12-13

Fund availability check, for control, 65, 73

Galileo, G., 29

Gardner, M., 7

General funds, and volume and cost analysis, 104-110

Ginsberg, S. G., 122

Governance, collegial, and conservatism, 28-29

Governmental Accounting Standards Board, 118

Higher education: financial management factors in, 12-16; fiscal crisis responses in, 120-122

Hopkins, D. S. P., 116

Horngren, C. T., 119

Hughes, G. C., 77

Hughes, K. S., 120

Hyatt, J. A., 7, 121

Information: collecting and reporting, 69-70; review of, 54-55, 101-104; technology for, 115-117

Institution: budget for, 44-49; financial plan for, 55; mission of, 104

Jenny, H. H., 77

Joint products: in higher education management, 13-14; and program unit budget, 53

Jossey-Bass, publications of, 117

Kerr, C., 29

Lisensky, R., 30, 31*n*

McClenney and McClenney, 30, 31

Management. *See* Financial management

Market demand, and cost analysis, 102-103, 107, 108

Massey, W. F., 116

Meisinger, R. J., Jr., 21, 58, 122

Mets, L. A., 124

Miles, R. E., Jr., 3

Mingle, J. R., 122

Mission, organizational, and cost analysis, 104

Mixed costs, concept of, 97

National Association of College and University Business Officers (NACUBO): and budgeting, 43, 57; and cost analysis, 96, 97; Financial Management Committee of, 5-6, 7, 8; as professional association, 117, 120, 121

National Center for Higher Education Management Systems, 117

Newton, I., 29

Nonprofit status, and higher education management, 14-15

Norris, D. M., 30

Obligations: in financial statements, 119; one-time and recurring, 78-80, 90-91

Opportunity costs, and reallocation, 107, 109

Payment, timely, for control, 67

Peat, Marwick, Mitchell, and Company, 96, 117, 120

Peterson, M. W., 124

Philosophy, utopian, and higher education management, 15-16

Planning: budgeting linked with, 28-35, 82-83; strategic, 29-33; as zero-sum game, 29, 32. *See also* Financial plan

Planning, programming, and budgeting systems (PPBS), 58

Poulton, N. L., 30

Professionalism, and higher education management, 16

Program administrators: competence of, 122–126; and control, 69–70; decision making by, 125; and financial plan, 56; and projections, 26–28; and recurring budgets, 81; responsibilities of, 19–20; roles of, 124–125; and technical experts, 123–124; and volume and general fund support, 104–110

Program units: budgets for, 49–54; cost-revenue relationships in, 99–101, 111–114; as educational enterprises, 4; financial improvement for, 108–109; financial management viewed by, 3–4; financial plan for, 55; and impact on other programs, 104, 109; reviewing and negotiating financial plans of, 56; service levels of, 83–84, 87, 92–93; status quo maintained for, 109–110; and strategic planning, 32

Projections: assessing factors for, 23–42; background on, 23–24; budgeting and planning linked for, 28–35; case studies of, 36–42; and institutional decisions, 25–26; of needs, opportunities, and adjustments, 24–28; and program administrators, 26–28; reasonable, 77–78; and uncontrollable factors, 24–25, 26–27

Purchasing office, central, for control, 67–68, 73–74

Rao, R. K. S., 6

Ray, H. W., 96

Reallocation decisions: cost analysis for, 94–114; savings and income for, 105–108; strategies for, 101

Receiving services, central, for control, 67

Recurring obligations and revenues, and asset base, 78–80, 90–91

Resources: acquiring, 44–47; for consumption requirements, 82; designated, 46, 47, 52–53, 118, 119; ensured, for high-priority activities, 82–83; responsibility for generating, 84; spending, 48–49; unrestricted, 46–47, 48–49, 51

Revenues: alternative, 103; collection of, for control, 68; quest for, 10–11; recurring and one-time, 78–80, 90–91. *See also* Costs and revenues

Robinson, D. D., 96

Santiago, A. A., 7, 121

Sheehan, B. S., 116

Shulman, C. H., 121

Society for College and University Planning, 117

States: illusory control by, 87–89; lotteries in, and one-time revenues, 79; partial-year funding by, 80; and unit costs, 95–96

Steeples, D. W., 121

Strategic planning: benefits and drawbacks of, 32–33; and projections, 29–33

Support services: as public utilities, 5; review mechanisms for, 84

Turk, F. J., 96

Unit costs: deviant, factors in, 102; emphasis on, 95–96; relationships of, 98–99

Units. *See* Program units

Vandament, W. E., 121

Variable costs: concept of, 97; and fixed costs, 103–104, 108; and reallocation, 107; relationships of, 98–99

Venture capital, for high-priority initiatives, 81–82

Volume, costs and revenues related to, 95–99, 104–111

Walker, D. E., 125